YOUR

Reflection

GOD

Your Reflection Your God

"Art To Reflect Yourself For Successful Future Through Mathematics, Science, and Analytics.............!"

By, A Scientific Thinker

Dr. Raghavendra Prasad MG

Copyright © <2023> <Dr. Raghavendra Prasad MG>

About Author

Dr. Raghavendra Prasad MG is a Software Professional, Trainer, and a Technical Writer with over 20+ years of experience in IT Industry. One of his popular technical books is **'Learning Selenium Testing Tools.'** Currently, he works for one of the biggest IT industries in India as Enterprise Architect –Automation.

His educational background includes an Engineering degree in Electronics & Communications, an MBA in Marketing and a Doctorate in Industrial Relations.

In his free time, he endeavors to explore the purpose of life. The quotes from Buddha, 'Everything happens for a reason,' and Krishna's saying, 'You are today (Present) because of your Yesterday's (Past) Decision,' & 'Current state subject to change' have elevated his thinking beyond the common man's level.

If 'Everything happens for a reason' holds true, then there must be underlying logical and analytical aspects that govern our lives. Conversely, reversing Buddha's saying, as Lord Krishna's message also holds true. The reasons behind these occurrences may be rooted in science, mathematics, and analytics, offering the potential to change the course of one's life.

We can shape our future through the right thought processes and decisions made in our day-to-day lives (in the present moment). By applying mathematical, scientific, and analytical methods or ways of thinking, we have the ability to change our future and achieve success in life.

How? The answer is in this book!

DEDICATION

This book is dedicated to my beloved wife, **Manasa**, who has been my strength and inspiration throughout life's journey.

She has supported me every step of the way, motivated me in every moment to climb the ladder of my dreams, and encouraged me to share my thoughts and learnings with all of you through this book.

Her presence in my life has made this book possible.

Thanks

Index

PREFACE

In the journey of my four-plus decades of life, I have encountered various situations and circumstances, faced a wide variety of challenges and gained numerous insights through my experiences. Initially, I wanted to create a set of notes that could serve as a sort of "**Constitution Book**" for my children & future descendants of my family. Later I thought to share my learning to everyone.

The quotes from Buddha, **"Everything happens for a reason"**, and Krishna's saying, **"You are today (Present) because of your Yesterday's (Past) Decision"**, & **"Current state subject to change"** has made me to think beyond.

If 'Everything happens for a reason' holds true, then there must be underlying logical and analytical aspects that govern our lives. Conversely, reversing Buddha's saying, as Krishna message is also holds true. The reasons behind these occurrences may be rooted in science, mathematics, and analytics, offering the potential to change the course of one's life.

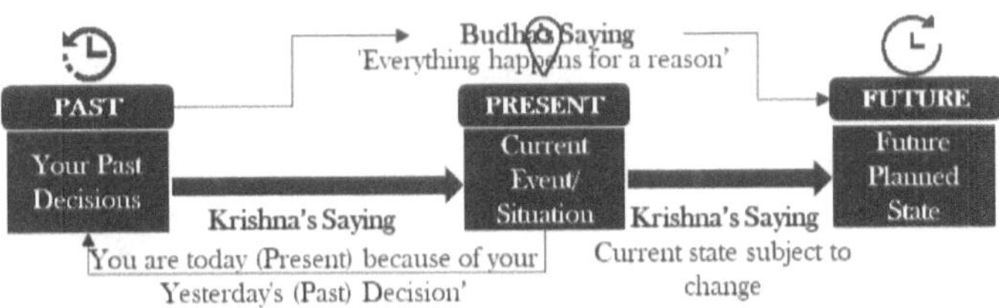

I came to realize the wisdom in Buddha's saying, 'Everything happens for a reason,' and Krishna's saying, 'You are today (Present) because of your Yesterday's (Past) Decision.' & 'Current state subject to change' - **based on the decisions you make today.**

My journey led me to ponder the underlying logic behind the events that unfold in an individual's life. As I observed the lives of many people at a high level, numerous questions arose within me. Here are a few of those questions:

- Why do some people find happiness while others do not?
- What causes some individuals to exude calmness and composure, while others exhibit harshness and arrogance?
- Why do some people attribute their experiences to luck, while others do not?
- What makes certain individuals confident, while others struggle with self-assurance?
- Why do some individuals perceive themselves as fortunate, while others do not share this sentiment?
- We can find people who are prosperous, restless, sad, calm, confused, motivated, with Gratitude, Empathy, Anxiety And so on states...!

These questions have sparked my exploration into the intricate web of life's mysteries and the underlying reasons for the diverse experiences that shape us.

I understand your curiosity and the desire to understand the underlying mathematical or scientific reasons behind life's outcomes. It's a common human inclination to seek patterns, reasons, and control over various aspects of life. However, it's essential to recognize that life is incredibly complex, and there may not always be a one-size-fits-all scientific or mathematical formula to explain every outcome.

Life's outcomes are influenced by a complex interplay of factors, including genetics, environment, personal choices, experiences, opportunities, and sometimes even elements beyond our comprehension. While mathematics and science can help us understand certain aspects of life, such as probabilities and patterns, the entirety of human existence is a multifaceted phenomenon that may not always fit neatly into equations or scientific models.

Nonetheless, the pursuit of knowledge and understanding is a noble one. It can lead to personal growth, self-awareness, and the development of strategies to navigate life's challenges. Keep in mind that while we may not always have complete control over external circumstances, we can often control our responses to them. This can be a powerful tool in shaping the outcomes we desire.

Ultimately, the search for answers regarding the reasons behind life's twists and turns can be a lifelong journey, and the knowledge and wisdom gained along the way can be as valuable as the destination itself.

I was just curious to understand the math or scientific reason behind it so that we can control it and shape the outcome as we wish. Many of you are also seeking answers for this. I started exploring the life stories of successful people, spiritual leaders, and monks can indeed provide valuable insights and inspiration, but could not arrive at a generic conclusion.

Even I have read thoughts from Chanakya's Artha Shastra, DVG's 'Manku Thimmana Kagga,' Basavanna's 'Vachanagalu,' Kanakadasa's 'Padagalu,' Sarvagnana's 'Vachanagalu,' Bhagavad-Gita sayings, etc., in an attempt to understand the mathematics behind the state of every person. I have been able to glean or predict some insights from this overall understanding, but not entirely. There is still confusion and unanswered questions lingering in my mind.

Later, I tried to understand the laws of nature, including Darwin's theory, genetic evolution, and instinctual behaviour of animals, among other things, in various situations. Fundamentally, all animals fight for food or gene transfer; nothing much.

Humans are different. Everyone's purpose in life is distinct immediately after the fulfilment of basic needs (Food, Shelter). Fundamentally, survival can be broken down into several key aspects:

- **Financial Security or Freedom**: The pursuit of money, which provides us with financial stability and the freedom to live life on our terms.
- **Identity**: The quest to understand who we are as individuals and establish our unique identity in the world. (Usually, people tend to transition from pursuing financial security to seeking a deeper sense of identity. This progression is common in life.)
- **Service to Others**: Though rare, some individuals find purpose in serving others, whether it be through acts of kindness, charity, or mentorship.
- **Service to Nature**: A commitment to preserving and protecting the environment and the natural world.
- **Service to Animals**: Compassion and care for the well-being of animals, often seen in animal rescue or advocacy.
- **Achievement in a Specific Field**: Striving for excellence and recognition in a particular area, such as sports, politics, business, entertainment, and more.
- Typically, individuals from middle or lower-middle-class backgrounds pursue education to secure a stable job, get married, raise children, and later focus on providing for their offspring's well-being.

However, it's essential to recognize that the above aspects are not the same as understanding the true purpose of life. They are more like desires, responsibilities, comforts, or needs and wants, all centered around an individual's protection & well-being. The problem arises when people confuse these pursuits with the ultimate purpose of life.

Having spent countless hours in introspection over many years, I've come to realize that an individual's thought process / mindset right decision in past play a significant role in determining their current life situation and status. Success is elusive until one aligns their mindset with the pursuit of success.

How to change your future state & status through a mathematical, scientific & analytical ways of thinking to achieve success in life is clearly explained in this book.

To summarize the concept or to make it clearer, I have tried to explain the concept in a very simplified manner, on how does your future is decided through mathematics, Science & Analytics.

Here is an example,

Let's consider three parameters: X, Y, and Z. The relationship between these parameters can be expressed through various mathematical operations, resulting in different interpretations – as shown below,

Case#1: $X + Y = Z$ 'Z is the Sum of X & Y
Case#2: $X * Y = Z$ 'Z is the Product of X & Y
Case#3: $X\%Y = Z$ 'Z is the % of X & Y
Case#4: $X - Y = Z$ 'Z is the Deference of X & Y
Case#5: $X / Y = Z$ 'Z is the Quotient of X & Y
Case#6: $X<>Y = Z$ 'Z is the Average of X & Y

.

Etc.

These equations represent different mathematical operations applied to X and Y, resulting in the value Z. Each case provides a unique interpretation of the relationship between these parameters.

If you look at the above cases, Assuming X and Y are Variables as of now, based on the Arithmetic Operators the result Z would change.

You can imagine how X, Y, Z Parameters and Arithmetic Operators are related to you,

You & Your Present State:
1. X is nothing but You as a person/ human being
2. Y is nothing but the Your Circumstances, Current State & Situation, etc.
3. In between X & Y the Arithmetic Operator is nothing but your mindset or how do you handle to the situation.

Your Future State:
4. Z is nothing but your Future state or Result, what you are going to get based on the input value of parameters X, Y & Arithmetic Operator you apply in between X & Y.

(As shown clearly in the below diagram)

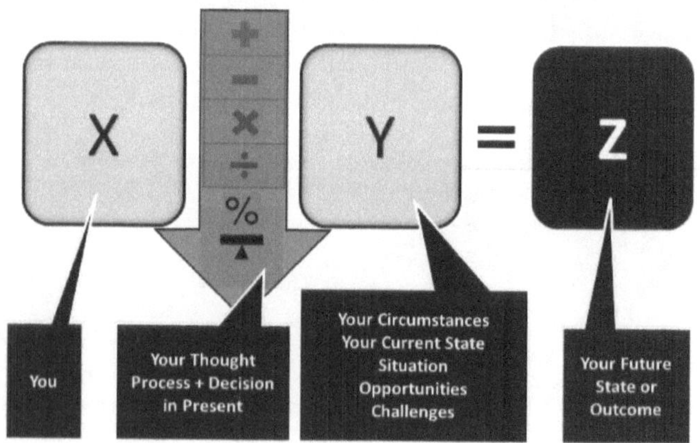

The below diagram is Expanded to show how the Mathematical, Science & Art is co- related in deciding your future.:

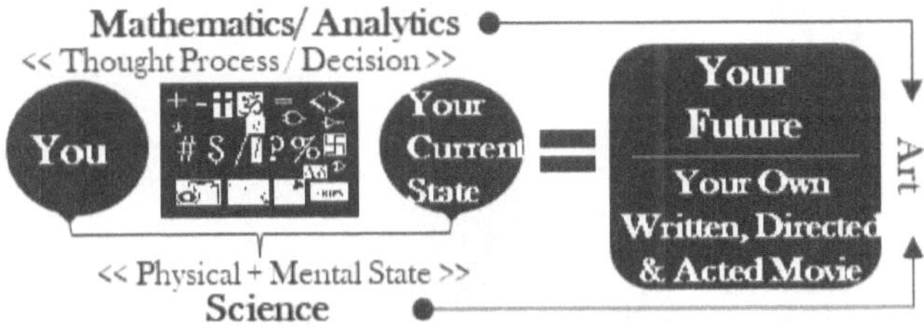

In this book, we delve into the question of how to navigate the parameters of 'You' (X) and your current state (Y) through a scientific approach to thinking. We introduce the idea of using a "mathematical operator" as a metaphorical representation of your thought process and decision-making. By applying these operators effectively, you can transform your future (Z) to align with your desired outcomes and aspirations. This book offers practical insights into leveraging this unique perspective to shape the path you want to follow in life.

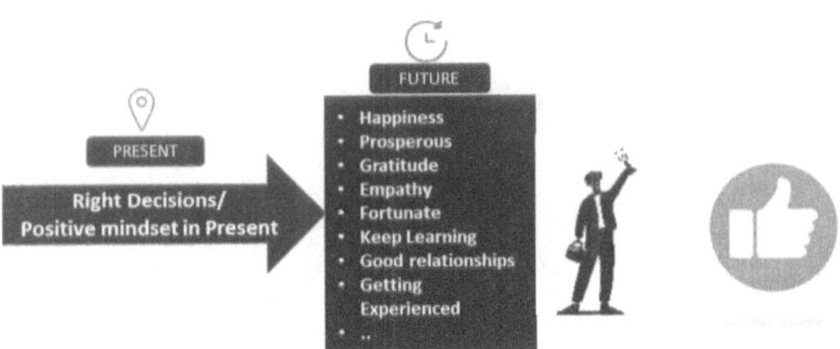

You might initially believe that your current state (Y) is beyond your control. However, as you begin to apply the principles outlined in this book and gain a deeper understanding of yourself (X), you'll come to realize that Y can indeed be influenced, planned, and intentionally designed to align with your expectations and goals. This book will guide you in harnessing your inner potential and shaping your current circumstances to create the future you desire.

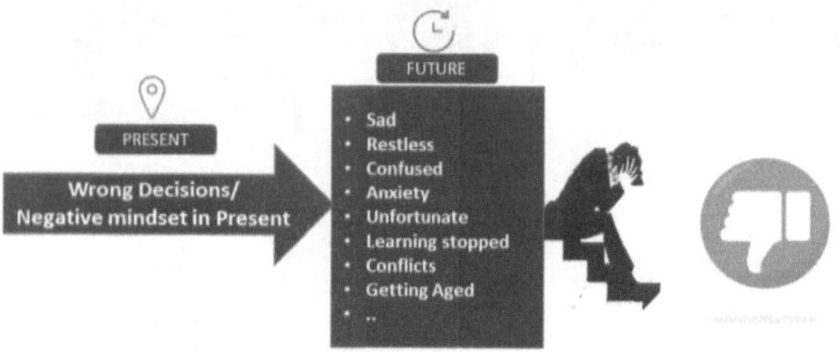

As "**The world is nothing but the reflection of your own thoughts.**"

The saying "ನೀ ಮಾಯೆಯೋ ನಿನ್ನೊಳು ಮಾಯೆಯೋ | ನೀ ದೇಹ ದೊಳಗೋ ನಿನ್ನೊಳು ದೇಹವೋ" (Nee maaye yo ninnolu maaye yo | Nee deha dolago ninnolu dehavo) **in** Kannada language by poet and philosopher Kanakadasa. Means, "**Are you the illusion, or is the illusion within you**" in other way round it gives below meaning as well.
"You are not just in the universe; you are a universe within"

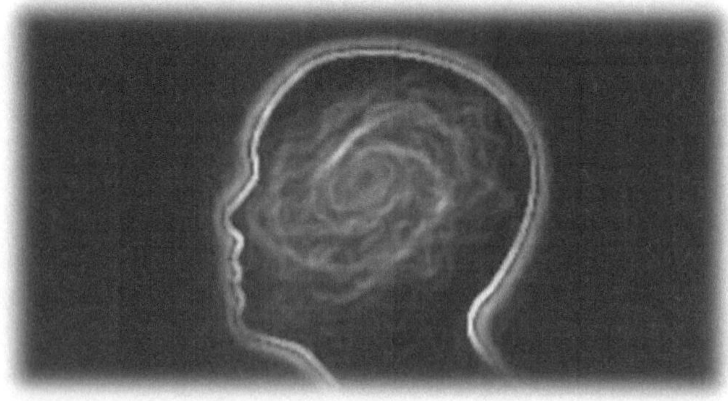

detailing out the sayings further,

Is an individual is caught in the illusion of the materialistic world (maya) or does the illusion resides within the individual.

It straightaway points one to introspect and gets in to deeper understanding of the nature of existence and the self.

Applying the right thought and decision, similar to using the principles of mathematics, is similar to responding with the correct thought process to various situations. This approach will lead to the desired future state (Z) that you have planned and envisioned. In essence, this book teaches you how to strategically navigate life's challenges by using a calculated and purposeful mindset to shape the outcomes you seek.

> **"Your Future is nothing but your own Written, Directed and Acted Movie."**
> **~Raghavendra Prasad MG**

"The best way to predict your future is to create it."

Summary could be depicted as follows,

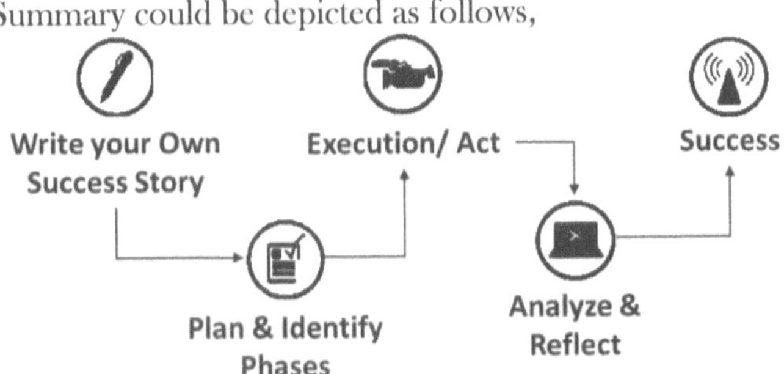

This book is about the art of crafting a successful future in alignment with your aspirations. Its primary goal is to facilitate your comprehension of life's purpose, enabling you to pursue your objectives without the burden of stress or disruptions to your personal life. The ultimate outcome is a life marked by improved health, tranquillity, happiness, prosperity, longevity, and contentment, all attained through the practice of sound decision-making within your present state of mind.

"Success is not the destination it's a continuous journey"
- Below is the depiction of Success Life Cycle,

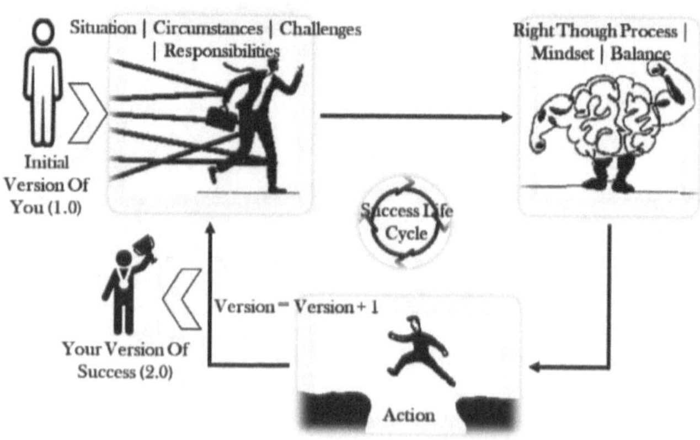

For whom is this book intended?

It's for those with a strong passion to achieve goals, those without influential connections or substantial support, those willing to work hard and make decisive choices in the present to reach greater heights in life.
As the saying goes, 'One best book is equal to a hundred good friends.' This book can be your best friend & also a good teacher, helping you understand the purpose of life and ascend the ladder of success.

"Please note that this is not a philosophical book. It's a guide offering actionable insights through Arts, Mathematical, Scientific, Analytical concepts to help you achieve success."

Wishing you all the best...!

As of now, please keep the following keywords in mind, as the path to success frequently involves these words:

Dream	Hard work
Vision	Good Intention
Goal	Preparation
Positive Mindset	Execution
Imagination	Iteration
Analize	Monitoring
Planning	Tracking
Role	Results / Success
Responsibilities	Celebration

Personal Notes & Learnings

CHAPTER #1:
You are living in a connected Universe

You are connected to the Universe and everything around. According to the current understanding of the universe, over 96% of the entire Universe is composed of the major four components: Hydrogen, Nitrogen, Oxygen, and Carbon. Similarly, our bodies also consist of these four elements, with the remaining 4% making up the rest of the elements.

Our Earth is filled with 75% water, and the same applies to our bodies as well.

The number & the complexity of neurons in our brain can be compared with the number of stars in the universe.

Please see the pictures below, which illustrate how our brain can be compared to the universe we live in.

Human Brain Cells - Observed in Ultramicroscope	Universe - Cluster of Galaxies: Seen from an Advanced Telescope
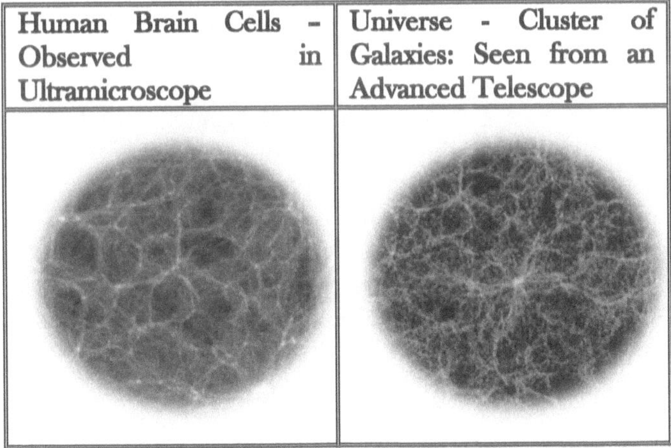	

These evidences clearly show, you are connected to the Universe and the Earth & You are the perfect design from the universe.

Let's explore the genetic similarities between humans and various other living beings:

- **Fruits** (e.g., Banana): We share approximately 60% of our DNA with them.
- **Fruit flies & Insects**: Approximately 65% genetic similarity.
- **Cows**: About 80% of our DNA is similar to cows.
- **Cats**: We share roughly 90% of our DNA with cats.
- **Dogs**: Our genetic similarity with dogs is approximately 94%.
- **Chimpanzees**: Surprisingly, we have a striking 98.8% genetic similarity with chimpanzees.
- **Humans**: Among humans, 99.9% of our genetic makeup is identical, and only 0.1% distinguishes us from each other. This difference is negligible and does not vary based on factors like religion (Hindu, Christian, Muslim, Sikh, Buddhist, etc.).

These genetic similarities highlight our shared ancestry with various species and underscore the unity of all living beings, emphasizing the importance of respecting and protecting the diversity of life on Earth.

We live in a connected universe where everything is interrelated—both the living and the non-living. We can view the Earth, the Sun, and the Universe as a single interconnected entity. This concept relates to physical connectivity.

Now, let's consider mental connectivity. Our observable universe spans approximately 100 billion light-years, which is equivalent to 9.46 trillion kilometres or 5.88 trillion miles. To reach our nearest star, Proxima Centauri, physically, we would need nearly 4.2 light-years.

However, our minds are not bound by space or time constraints, allowing them to reach any place instantaneously, mentally. That's the beauty of our minds;

they can travel anywhere without the limitations of time or space.

For instance, Albert Einstein never physically visited the Sun or used a telescope to understand what was happening there, yet he could describe precisely what was happening on the Sun, all through the power of his mind.

Similarly, Stephen Hawking never stood up from his wheelchair to comprehend the nature of our universe and formulate theories on black holes. He accomplished all of this through the power of his mind.

Isaac Newton articulated the Universal Laws of Gravitational Force through the power of his mind, without relying solely on physical measurements or calculations.

Swamy Tulsidas included an approximate reference to the distance between the Earth and the Sun in his Hanuman Chalisa mantra.

Our ancient Indian astrologers used to refer to Jupiter as Brihaspati, signifying its larger size. How did they conclude that Jupiter is larger than any other planet? They didn't have telescopes to physically see Jupiter. It was all possible due to the power of the mind.

You may have observed that animals become panicked and restless when an earthquake or flood is impending.

Likewise, you might have noticed that mothers, whether in the animal kingdom or among humans, feel discomfort when something goes wrong with their offspring or children even when they are not nearby.

In a similar vein, various techniques, both positive and negative, such as Chanting mantras/ switch words, Aura, Reiki, Black magic, or Voodoo, are practiced.

The same principle applies to our understanding of concepts like electromagnetism, quantum mechanics, and string theories. These can only be comprehended mentally because we cannot observe them physically.

An atom can be further divided into quarks and leptons. If you could separate them and keep them apart anywhere in the universe, they would tend to vibrate at the same frequency.

In conclusion, I want to convey to all of you that your mind is incredibly powerful. It possesses an enormous capacity to grasp the intricacies of the universe because it is connected both physically and mentally to everything in the cosmos.

"You are the reflection of the ultimate grand design and incredible, wonderful architecture of the Universe. You are so important; be proud of yourself."
~Raghavendra Prasad MG

The Universe and the world are nothing but the reflections of your own thoughts, nothing else.
It's similar to when you do any type of expression in front of a mirror; it will precisely mimic it back to you.

This is 100% true. You might not believe it or find it hard to believe right now, but eventually, when you change your thought process, you will start realizing it.

How to train your mind or Brain - we are going to discuss this in the following chapters.

Our Observable Universe:

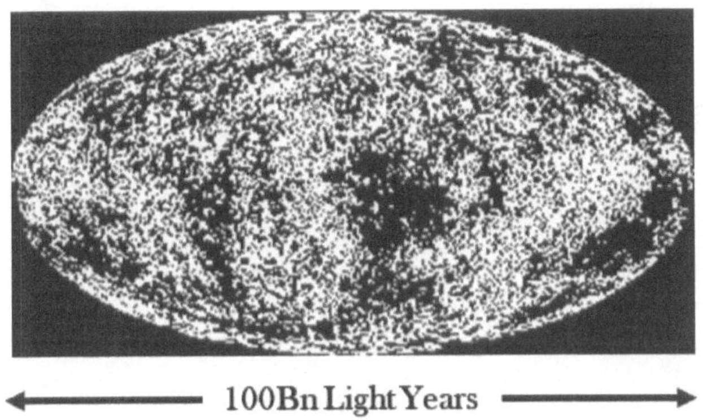

Couple of sayings from the experienced people, proverbs or philosophical teachings in the context of this chapter,

"Everything in the universe is within you. Ask all from yourself."

~Jalal al-Din Rumi

"We are all connected; to each other, biologically. To the Earth, chemically. To the rest of the universe, atomically."

~Neil deGrasse Tyson

"You are a mirror reflecting a noble face. This universe is not outside of you. Look inside yourself; everything that you want, you already are."

~Jalal al-Din Rumi

Personal Notes & Learnings

CHAPTER#2:
Good Luck & Fortune are just by Mindset Nothing else.

As I mentioned in the first chapter, where I stated that we are all equally connected and related to the universe and everything around us, there is no such thing as 'Good Luck' or 'Bad Luck,' 'Fortunate' or 'Unfortunate.' It's all in our Thought Process.

"Luck happens when preparation meets opportunity."
~Seneca

For example, there was once an experiment conducted in the UK to explore the concepts of good luck and bad luck. They gathered individuals who claimed to be lucky and an equal number who claimed to be unlucky. All of them were asked to sit in a hall and given a general question paper (a short story followed by some tricky questions based on the same story).

Closed-circuit cameras were installed to observe everyone's behaviour. Surprisingly, those who considered themselves lucky scored high marks, while those who believed they were unlucky scored lower.

When we observe these interesting facts on the camera...

People who feel lucky	People who feel unlucky
Confident	Unconfident
Patient	Impatient/ irritated
Organized/ Disciplined	Unorganized
Living in Present moment.	

Not worried about others, concentrating on their own. Not in Race Winning attitude Cleary went through the terms and conditions. Estimated the time accordingly. Cleary read the story and understand it by spending the considerable estimated amount of time, noted and highlighted the points. Went through the questions one by one and answered with no hurry. **Final Result:** Scored good marks	Not living in present moment, thinking on something else in mind. Worried about others answering in speed or hurry., In Race Defeating attitude Directly jumping to questions and trying to trace back the answers, get into confusion. Tried to answer the questions without understanding the story. Tried to answer all the questions in a hurry. **Final Result:** Scored less marks

It's just a math to become Lucky, as we do "Shift-Left" in software development by strictly adhering to the rules on the left side of the table mentioned above, you can become lucky.

This, in turn, boosts confidence, concentration, memory, observation, and the ability to perform tasks accurately and with perfection.

Conclusion:

It's not that people who feel lucky do not have any problems in life; it's all about how they deal with them.

In the situation mentioned above, let's assume the question paper represents a problem statement in daily life. How you deal with it is most important and determines whether you consider yourself lucky or unlucky. You decide whether you are fortunate or not. Start applying the steps that people who feel lucky applied while answering the questions.

(Clear Observation is like reading the question paper of your own life carefully – will lead to success & make you feel lucky)
Observation & understanding the present moment is the key that can lead you to fortune and success. Here are two examples illustrating the power of observation:

#1: Andre Agassi - The Art of Observation to Success

Tennis legend Andre Agassi achieved multiple world championships through the art of observation. He learned to outwit Boris Becker by keenly watching him. Agassi noticed that Becker's tongue movement correlated with the direction of his serve. This keen observation gave Agassi a crucial edge in defeating his opponent.

#2: Muhammad Ali - Learning through Observation to success

Muhammad Ali, originally a poor boy named Cassius Clay, rose to become a world boxing champion multiple times. His journey began when he watched a television boxing program called "Tomorrow's Champions" with unwavering attention. Through diligent observation and hard work, he went on to win an impressive 56 out of 61 fights in his lifetime, solidifying his status as a boxing legend.

These examples underscore the importance of paying close attention to details & using observation as a tool to excel in your chosen field.

> "The moment you feel you are lucky and fortunate – you are indeed lucky and fortunate."
> ~Raghavendra Prasad MG

"Lucky people accept failure as 'I failed,' (Ideal way of telling is Not Passed) while unlucky people tend to see failure as 'I am a failure."

> "The universe plays no favorites; it's the individual who decides to be lucky or unlucky based on their Thought Process."
> ~Raghavendra Prasad MG

> "If you feel you are fortunate you are right. If you feel you are unfortunate yes you are right."
> ~Raghavendra Prasad MG

Couple of sayings from the experienced people, proverbs or philosophical teachings in the context of this chapter,

"The harder I work, the luckier I get."
~Samuel Goldwyn

"I find that the harder I work, the more luck I seem to have."
~Thomas Jefferson

"Hard work is the key to success; luck is the door to opportunities."

"Luck can't be controlled, but hard work can be guaranteed."

"There's no substitute for hard work."
~Thomas Edison

"Hard work beats talent when talent doesn't work hard."
~Tim Notke

"Success is 1% inspiration, 99% perspiration."
~Thomas Edison

"Luck is not chance; it's toil. Fortune's expensive smile is earned."
~Emily Dickinson

"The best luck of all is the luck you make for yourself."
~Douglas MacArthur

"Luck is great, but most of life is hard work."
~Iain Duncan Smith

"Hard work is the foundation of all achievements."
~Lailah Gifty Akita

Personal Notes & Learnings

CHAPTER#3:
Trust that everything happens for a reason, and the outcome will be ultimately good.

"The Universe plays grand scheme of things, it's all for the best."

"The universe has a plan; you can't see it."
                    ~Thomas Campbell

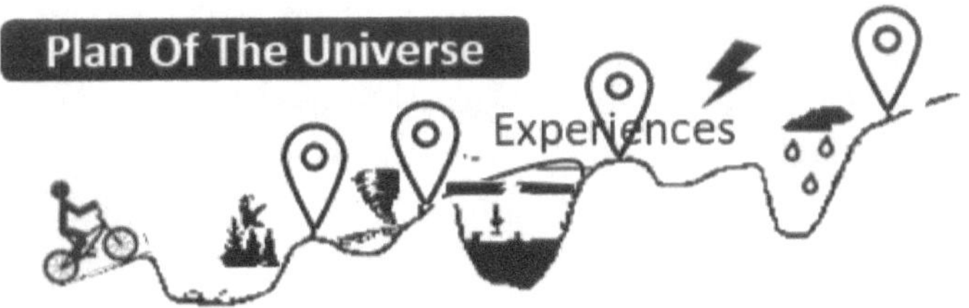

I would like to explain this chapter through two stories here.

Story #1: A King and His Minister
One day, a King and his Minister ventured into the jungle for a safari. The King was hunting a deer with his bow and arrow when he accidentally cut his fingers. He writhed in pain, and the Minister reassured him, saying, 'Don't worry,

Your Majesty. Everything happens for a reason, and the outcome is ultimately good.'

The King, however, became infuriated and retorted, 'I am suffering from pain, and you're telling me this is for my good? Do you comprehend the punishment for such words? You shall be imprisoned for a couple of months.' The Minister, with a serene smile, repeated, 'Everything happens for a reason, and the result is good.'

A week later, the King set out for another hunting expedition in the jungle. On his way, he was captured by a tribe who sought a human sacrifice for their goddess. They seized the King and prepared for the ritual. However, the Tribe's Priest noticed a wound on the King's hand and declared, 'We cannot sacrifice him; he bears a wound. We require a human without any fresh injuries on their body.' Consequently, they released the King.

Recalling the Minister's words, 'Everything happens for a reason, and the result is good,' the King returned to his palace and ordered the Minister's release. He apologized to his Minister for the unjust imprisonment, to which the Minister graciously replied, 'Do not fret, Your Majesty. Everything happens for a reason, and the outcome is good.' The King inquired how his imprisonment could be for the best, and the Minister elucidated, 'Had I not been in prison, you might have taken me into the jungle, and the Tribe would have captured us both. Since they couldn't sacrifice you due to your wound, they would have sacrificed me instead. Hence, 'Everything happens for a reason, and the result is good.'

You must firmly believe that whatever transpires in your life is ultimately for the best.

Story #2: A Chinese Farmer and His Horse

Once, there lived a Chinese farmer. He had a horse that he used for commuting and carrying things to his farm every day. One day, it ran away, and the neighbours came to his house, saying, "What an unfortunate event! It shouldn't have happened to you." The farmer remained calm and replied, "That's fine."

After a few days, the same horse returned with two other horses. The neighbours, astonished, visited the farmer again and exclaimed, "How fortunate you are! Now you have three horses!" The farmer responded, "That's fine."

Later, while riding the horse, the farmer son fell and got injured. The neighbours once more came, saying, "What an unfortunate thing happened! It shouldn't have happened to you." The farmer's reply remained the same, "That's fine."

In a couple of days, a war was declared by the king. The king of the territory asked for the participation of one youth from every household to save the nation. When the king's ministers came and saw the farmer's son with a wound, they said he couldn't participate in the war and left him. Again, the neighbours came to the farmer's house, saying, "How fortunate you are!" The farmer, as always, responded with, "That's fine."

If you observe, the strong belief of the farmer worked. Whatever happened was for the good only. It's all about having a strong trust in life and the universe.

The problem with every human being is that they want life to be as they expect it to be, instead of accepting it as it comes and strongly trusting that whatever happens is for the good only.

The above two stories clearly convey the message of what this chapter is all about.

You can visualize your own life, reflecting on moments that initially seemed negative but later revealed their positive outcomes.

Everyone encounters challenging times in life, whether it's **academic setbacks, career obstacles, job loss, health issues, business failures, financial Crisis, Recession, being rejected, trust factor, relationships, miss understandings, loss of identity or respect and many more.** It's all about those who maintain a positive mindset, as they are the ones who can transform these difficult experiences into valuable lessons and positive results.

"Tough times are Good which makes you strong & more valuable"

~ Raghavendra Prasad MG

"Same Stone can be under the foot or stand as a respectful Statue" Its all in your hands

Couple of sayings from the experienced people, proverbs or philosophical teachings in the context of this chapter,

"Every setback is a setup for a comeback."
~Joel Osteen

"Not getting what you want – something big is awaited."

"When one door closes, many doors open."
~Alexander Graham Bell

"Life will be of series of ups/ downs, curves/ turns, all leads to the right path."

"Trust the timing of your life."

"ಆಗುವುದೆಲ್ಲ ಒಳಿತೇ ಆಯಿತು" (Everything that happened is for good)
~Purandara Dasa

Personal Notes & Learnings

CHAPTER#4:
What's goes around comes around.

Sri Krishna says, "**Karma Returns**," which is nothing but "**What goes around comes around.**"

> **"Take account of yourselves before you are taken to account."**
>
> ~Extract From Quran

"For Every Action, there is an Equal & Opposite Reaction"
~Isaac Newton (3rd Law of Motion)

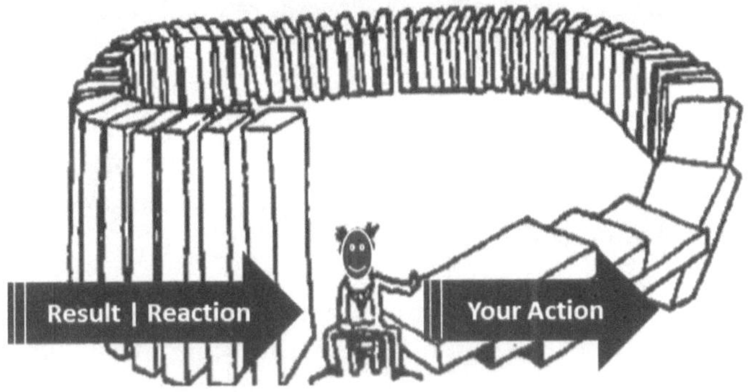

Story#1: This chapter is best explained through a story rather than theory and analysis. It's the famous tale of a poor Scottish farmer and his son. One day, as the farmer was on his way home, he heard a cry for help coming from a nearby lake. Without the second thought, he rushed to the lake and found a young boy drowning, screaming and struggling for his life. The farmer bravely saved the boy from a terrifying death.

The following day, a wealthy man visited the farmer's humble abode and introduced himself as the father of the boy he had rescued from drowning. He said, 'I wish to repay you for your heroic act. You saved my son's life.' The poor farmer humbly responded, 'I cannot accept payment for doing what was right.' At that moment, the farmer's own son appeared at the door. 'Is this your son?' the rich man inquired. 'Indeed,' the poor farmer proudly replied. The wealthy man then proposed, 'Allow me to provide him with an education equal to that of my own son. I am confident he will grow into a man of whom we both can be proud.' True to his word, he did just that.

The farmer's son received an education at the finest schools and eventually graduated from St. Mary's Hospital Medical School in London, gaining worldwide renown as Sir Alexander Fleming, the discoverer of penicillin.

Years later, the same wealthy man's son, the one saved from the lake, fell ill with pneumonia. What saved his life this time? Penicillin. The wealthy man's name was Lord Randolph Churchill, and his son was none other than Sir Winston Churchill.

This story beautifully illustrates how the farmer's virtuous deed led to an education for his son, while the wealthy man's act of providing education resulted in a second chance at life for his own son. It unquestionably upholds the principle of 'What goes around comes around.

Story#2: This is an incident that happened in my life exclusively. It was around the years 2006-07 when one of my friends' bosses lost his job and decided to set up his own firm. He needed certain inputs and training to be conducted in his new venture, and I willingly assisted him without expecting anything in return.

Later, in 2009, during the recession caused by the Lehman Brothers' impact, I found myself without a job. It was during this difficult time that the same person I had helped earlier came to my aid, helping me secure a job. This personal experience served as strong evidence of the principles outlined in this chapter.

The 2 previous stories focused on positive karma returning, but now let's explore some examples of negative karma effects.,

Story#3: There once was a stingy, wealthy businessman whose father fell seriously ill. The doctors recommended a surgery that would cost a significant amount of money. After extensive calculations, the rich man concluded that it was not worth performing the surgery on his father. He was not only concerned about the medical expenses but also decided to let his father die.

One day, the businessman took matters into his own hands and ended his father's life by squeezing his neck. This act was witnessed by his own son.

Twenty years later, the businessman found himself in a similar situation to that of his father's. He faced consequences strikingly similar to what he had done to his own father, demonstrating how negative karma can return over time.

Story#4: This is an incident that happened to one of my elderly friends, who is a lawyer by profession. He used to share this unfortunate incident that occurred in his life. At the time, he had a small baby boy who was about 9 months old and suffering from severe fever. It was around 9 PM in the evening, and my friend rushed to a nearby clinic. The doctor at the clinic was about to leave for her home, and she was in a hurry. She didn't take much time to diagnose the child. Instead, she administered an injection to the 9-month-old child's left arm, who tragically passed away due to the pain in his arm.

Two decades later, the doctor's daughter, who was residing in the US, was pregnant. However, both she and the baby tragically died during delivery. In this case, it appeared that negative karma had returned, might be co-incidence as well.

My friend used to tell me that the doctor couldn't escape the pain of losing a child in front of the parents.

I personally believe that the universe involves complex calculations beyond a common man thinking & understanding.
It's always better to practice doing good and being good in life, regardless of the consequences that may unfold.

The result and output can also be correlated or predicted with Table #Positive Mindset from CHAPTER #8 as well.

Karma is a law by nature – **"Bird eat ants, and when the bird dies, ants eat the bird."**

Couple of sayings from the experienced people, proverbs or philosophical teachings in the context of this chapter,

"What you give is what you receive" | "You reap what you sow"

"What you have done to others will come back to you."

"It's the law of cause and effect" | "Actions have consequences"

These sayings all convey the idea that the actions and decisions you make in life will eventually have consequences, whether positive or negative, that will return to you in some way.

Personal Notes & Learnings

Personal Notes & Learnings

CHAPTER#5:
Free up your mind from problems & disappointments

"Problems are not stop signs; they are guidelines."
~Robert H. Schuller

As I mentioned in the previous chapters, according to the laws and principles of the universe, we are all part of the grand design. Each individual is equally interconnected and related, both mentally and physically, to the universe.

"You are the owner & reason for your problems and disappointments...!"
~Raghavendra Prasad MG

If you're feeling disappointed and believe that unfavourable events have occurred in your life, it's important to recognize that you may be the primary cause of these circumstances. Instead of engaging in a blame game, take a moment to understand the situation.

Avoid thinking, like 'I'm facing this problem because of him/her.' Instead, dedicate some time to introspection and try to identify the root cause of the issue and its implications. Shift your focus towards finding solutions and ways to overcome the challenges, rather than dwelling on the losses.

When you're trying to understand the problems you've faced, you'll likely realize that your source of disappointment falls under one or more of the following reasons:
- Making decisions hastily.
- Holding blind beliefs.

- Allowing situations to control you instead of the other way around.
- Letting emotions take over.
- Outcomes not meeting expectations.
- Dealing with someone who doesn't align with your expectations.
- Seeking quick profits through shortcuts.
- Failing to recognize long-term impacts.
- Failed to identify Fake or Wrong People
- Overlooking losses on the flip side.
- Becoming excessively selfish.
- Intentionally causing harm to someone (either mentally or, in rare cases, physically).
- Hurting someone's ego.
- Ignorance.
- Excessive trust.
- Laziness.
- Greediness.
- Jealousy.
- Selfishness.
- Fear.
- Possessiveness.
- Excessive expectations (a major source of disappointment).
- Negative thoughts.
- Overconfidence.
- Overthinking.
- Guilt.
- Over Protection
- Insecurity
- lack of confidence
- and so on....!

Examples could be,

- Pursuing short-term or instant pleasures, such as drugs, casual sex, or alcohol.
- Blindly investing in the hope of high returns or quick profits.

- Placing excessive trust in someone or investing impulsively in funds, money lending, or real estate.
- Sharing your weaknesses or those of your family members with someone you trust, who may exploit this information later on.
- Neglecting minor issues in your home life, which could escalate into significant problems in the future, or disregarding lengthy conversations with a son or daughter that may become problematic later.
- Holding unrealistic expectations for your life or someone else's, leading to disappointment and subsequent suffering.

Reason for Depression:
I've noticed that wealthier individuals tend to experience depression more often than those with fewer financial resources. This could be attributed to their heightened expectations, both from life and the people around them.

"Expectation Leads to Suffering."
~**Buddha**

I would say, **"Emotions give rise to Expectations, which leads to Disappointment than finally end result is Suffering."**

Mathematical formula for Disappointment is as follows,

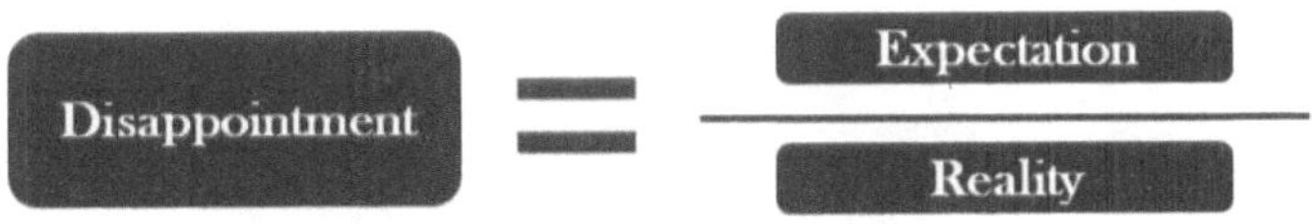

If you can categorize your problems or reasons for disappointment among the factors listed above, I assure you that by shifting your mindset, you can find solutions and progress towards a successful, confident, prosperous, and happier life. How you can achieve this will be explored in the following chapters.

Easy Steps to Handle Any Problem:

- **Step #0**: First, differentiate whether the problem is truly yours or not. If it's your problem, proceed to the next step.
- **Step #1**: Accept the problem without assigning blame.
- **Step #2**: Assess whether the problem is solvable. If it's not, consider leaving it as it is. If it is solvable, move on to the next step.
- **Step #3**: Identify the solution, duration to solve the problem, investment required (Time, Energy, Money), impact, Potential losses to implement it, take a calculative decision and proceed accordingly.

Same is as shown in the below diagram,

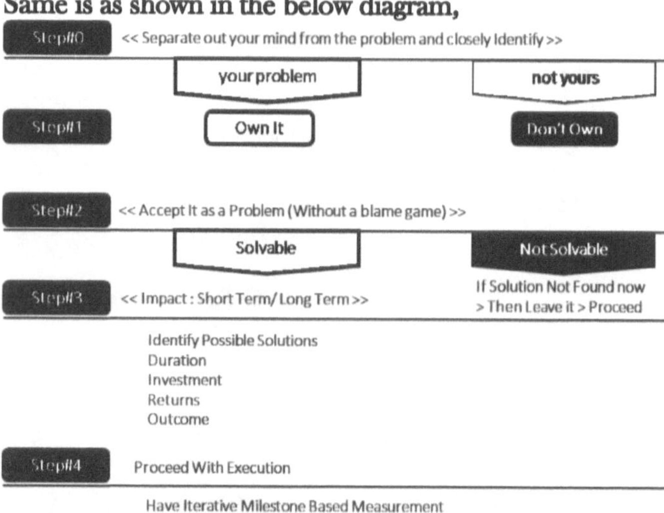

Note: I'm not suggesting that you should ignore or avoid responding to others' problems. If a problem doesn't belong to you, refrain from assuming ownership. Instead, offer assistance and guidance to help them solve it.

Ultimately, the responsibility for solving a problem should rest with its rightful owner. Taking ownership on someone else's issues can lead to personal difficulties, raise in expectations and a loss of inner peace.

For instance, if your child is struggling with mathematics, it's crucial not to assume ownership of their problem. Instead, seek ways to assist and support them in achieving success. Similarly, when faced with someone else's problems, avoid taking ownership. Instead, provide guidance and assistance, allowing them to take control and work towards a solution. Remember, **owning others problem may lead to a never-ending cycle of dependency**.

Another common scenario is when an adult, like a married daughter, approaches her affluent father with relationship issues. While the father can offer moral, financial, and emotional support, it's essential not to take ownership of her problem. Ownership of the problem should rest with the daughter, and she must seek help, support, and suggestions from loved ones to resolve it herself.

It's a law by nature:

"Individuals must take ownership of the problems they face."

~Raghavendra Prasad MG

Many may have witnessed how elephant calves must stand up shortly after birth. If they fail to do so, their mother might kick them, and if they still can't stand, the parent may abandon them, leaving them to die.

If you believe that a problem is currently unsolvable, it's best not to dwell on it excessively, as there may be limited actions you can take. Instead, set it aside and direct your attention towards your upcoming life goals. In time, many problems tend to resolve themselves, decrease in intensity, or you may adapt to living with them.

Keep in mind that the lifespan of most problems is typically shorter than your own lifespan, Problems often appear smaller when you elevate yourself and view them from a

broader perspective or over period of time; in some cases, they even diminish.

– as shown in the below diagram,

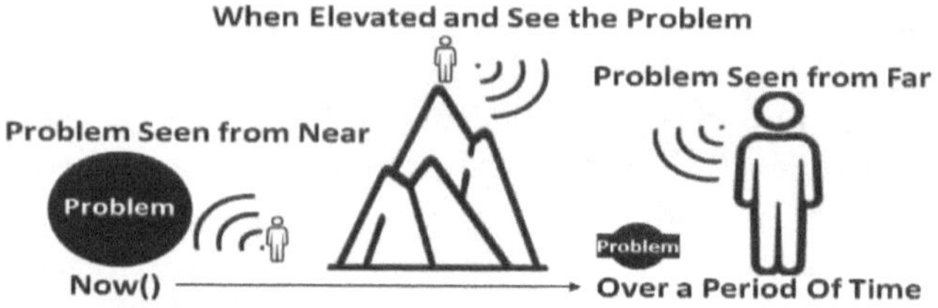

> **Stay Calm, peaceful in any kind of situation**
> When you become irritated with the situation around you, the Universe tends to exacerbate the situation, leading to even more frustration. Conversely, when you maintain a calm demeanour amidst challenging circumstances, the Universe often responds by bringing about a sense of tranquillity and improving the situation.
>
> This observation is a common thread in the experiences of people of all ages, from children to the elderly.

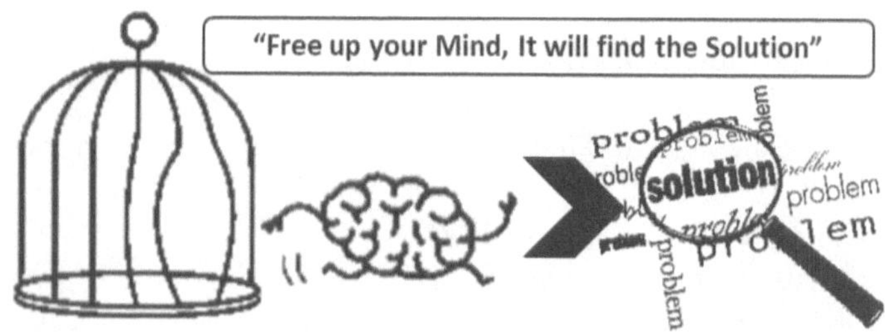

"It's a law of nature that rain, storms, or earthquakes won't persist indefinitely; they eventually calm down. Similarly, your mind should also find a state of calmness regardless of the situation you're facing. You cannot sustain a state of disturbance for long. Imagine if rain, storms, or earthquakes were to occur continuously for a year – the impact would be immense."

"You don't get perfect things in this world, but you have to make it perfect."

"Invest Energy & Time cautiously to solve your problems"
~Raghavendra Prasad MG

"You are both the cause and the remedy for your problems and disappointments."
~Raghavendra Prasad MG

"The universe presents problems & challenges in accordance with an individual's capabilities. Just as an elephant has its own set of challenges, so does an ant."
~Raghavendra Prasad MG

Couple of sayings from the experienced people, proverbs or philosophical teachings in the context of this chapter,

"Locks (Problems) are not created or manufactured without Keys (Solutions)"
~Dr. Thomas Gordon

"Taking ownership of your problems is the first step towards finding solutions."

"Life becomes easier when you own your problems."
"Your problems are like your baggage; carry them based on the priority & the choice you make."

"Blaming others for your problems is like running away from your responsibility."

"A problem is a chance for you to do your best."

"Own your problems, or they are going to own you"

"Tough time creates Strong Men, Strong Men creates Easy Times, Easy Times create Weak Men, Weak Men create Tough Times."

~G. Michael Hopf

"The greatest glory in living lies not in never falling, but in rising every time we fall."

~Nelson Mandela

"Every adversity, every failure, every heartache carries with it the seed of an equal or greater benefit."

~Napoleon Hill

"Success is not final; failure is not fatal: It is the courage to continue that counts."

~Winston Churchill

"The problem is not the problem; the problem is your attitude about the problem."

~Jack Sparrow

"In the middle of every difficulty lies opportunity."
~Albert Einstein

Personal Notes & Learnings

Personal Notes & Learnings

CHAPTER#6:
Work for Passion, Enjoyment, & Pleasure; Ultimately to Achieve Financial Freedom.

"Choose a job you love, and you will never have to work a day in your life."

~Confucius

"Work is worship, worship is work."

~Basavanna

To begin, it's essential to understand that enjoyment is a relative term, shaped by individual perspectives.

Enjoyment can be described as a sensation of happiness within the brain or mind.

It can manifest both physically and mentally, yielding the same positive reaction in your brain.

Mental Enjoyment	Physical Enjoyment
	Smoking
	Alcohol
Sense	Family time
Wealth/Money	Socializing
Identity	Parties
Power	Reading
Piety	Sleeping
Malevolence	Benevolence
Cursing	Playing Games
Memory	Long Drives
Imagination	Traveling
Expectation	Listening to Music
Faking	Watching Movies
And so on...	Visiting Holy Places
	Intimate Relationships (Sex)
	And the list goes on...

Context Switching Is Vital:

One common issue with routine jobs is that people often become bored. The human brain craves variety and change.

For instance, someone who works in a park may find enjoyment in visiting a cinema theatre, Similarly, a person working in a cinema theatre might relish the experience of going to a park, sitting or walking beneath the trees.

This demonstrates how alternating environments and experiences can help alleviate the monotony of routine tasks.

Love Your Job!

Remember that your current job is not your final destination; it's a part of your life journey, offering valuable experiences. Your path in life is long, with countless achievements awaiting you.

No job is insignificant in this world; each plays a vital role. Your job exists because it's necessary, reflecting a business or a give-and-take relationship. You work, and in return, you receive compensation for your efforts.

Embrace each day with a positive mindset and approach your work with enthusiasm. Maintain a continuous learning attitude. Always ask yourself, 'How can I do this job differently? How can I improve efficiency and productivity?' Extend a helping hand to those in need, and set your sights on where you want to be in the next few years.

Continuously ponder how you can progress to the next level, both in terms of your position and your financial standing. With this attitude, you'll discover numerous avenues for personal and professional growth. Your perspective will shift, and you'll perceive the world as supportive of your development. This will also unlock your capacity for multi-dimensional thinking.

Financial Stability vs. Freedom

Financial stability holds paramount importance in life. It's evident that people earning Rs 10K – 25K in India or 2K – 3K USDs in the US per month can be happier than those earning Rs 50K or 5 - 8K USDs, respectively. It's all about your mindset and how effectively you manage your current resources. I'm not suggesting you shouldn't aspire for more.

No matter what you do, always keep financial freedom as your ultimate goal. It's the key to confidence and strength.

"Don't work for money; make money work for you."
~Robert Kiyosaki

This mindset shift can lead you towards a path of greater financial independence and empowerment.

Remember, your today's (Present) state is because of your Yesterday's (Past) decision and your tomorrow (Future) depends on your today's decisions.

Managing Finances Wisely

It's crucial to manage your finances thoughtfully, taking into account your current circumstances and lifestyle. Avoid the traps of competition, comparison, or unnecessary extravagance. **Live your life for yourself.**

Make a conscious effort to save for emergencies and refrain from taking loans unless absolutely necessary.

Remember that your financial well-being plays a significant role in job satisfaction. When you find contentment in every moment, your mind will function differently, enabling you to envision and execute plans to achieve your future goals.

Your Needs vs. Your Wants

Much like the term 'ENOUGH,' the concepts of Needs and Wants are relative and highly dependent on your financial situation. What constitutes a 'need' varies greatly from person to person.

For a super-rich individual, a luxury cruise or a private flight might be considered a need, while a space station remains a want. Wealthy individuals might see a helicopter as a need, while a super-luxury flight is a want. Conversely, for someone in the lower middle class, a two-wheeler is a need, and a car is a want.

Digging deeper, for a daily wage worker, a bicycle is a need, and a two-wheeler is a want. For a person who begs on the street, food is a necessity, while shelter becomes a luxury. The perception of needs and wants varies from one person's circumstances to another.

It's essential not to compare yourself to others. Live your life on your terms, as no one else is responsible for it. Show-offs and comparisons usually yield no real benefits and can lead to significant losses for you.

Hence, when considering any investment, it's crucial to ask yourself the following questions:

- Is it truly necessary for me?
- How frequently will I use this?
- Why is it of such importance?
- What is the specific purpose behind this purchase?
- How will I make use of it?
- What potential outcomes can I anticipate?
- What will be the impact of this investment?
- What are the associated maintenance costs?

- Can my current financial situation comfortably accommodate the payments?

If you can provide satisfactory answers to all these questions, then proceed with your investment. Otherwise, it's advisable to apply a brake and reconsider.

Follow 8:8:8 Rule! Without FAIL

What is this 8:8:8 Rule, see the below table?

<< Total – 24 Hours a Day >> Spend time as if the more expensive than Money, you can earn Money at any point of time in your life, but you can't buy time with any amount of money.		
HEALTH **<< 8 Hours >>**	**WORK** **<< 8 Hours >>**	**RESPONSIBILITIES** **Then** **RELATIONSHIPS** **<< 8 Hours >>**
Prioritize early bedtime and morning wake-up (with a mandatory 6 hours of deep sleep). Cultivate good dietary habits. Foster positive thinking habits. Steer clear of junk food. Exercise control over Smoking & alcohol consumption. Stay mindful of your physical well-	Establish your current baseline. Visualize your future or desired state. Define short-term goals and actively pursue them. Set long-term objectives and work steadily toward achieving them. Strategize and plan your actions. Prepare a step-by-step approach. Execute your plans.	**Start with your responsibilities; genuine relationships will naturally follow.** Recognize that satisfying relationships aren't built on expensive gifts or lavish spending; it's an endless pursuit. Set realistic expectations, especially when it comes to spending. Respond to emotions and prioritize needs over wants.

being and health status. **Dedicate at least 30 Minutes a day to self-reflection, for within yourself lies the opportunity to converse with an amazing person in the world.**	Reflect on your progress. Seek and incorporate feedback. Commit to continuous improvement. Gauge success through periodic milestones. Above all, maintain agility—be ready to adapt to change. **Make sure you are Working for Both Professional and Financial Growth.**	Avoid exceeding your limits, as it can disrupt the balance of your 8:8:8 Rule, leading to work-related stress and health issues. Incorporate daily exercise and walks into your routine to stay fit. Maintain personal hygiene and dress well, as being well-dressed reflects discipline. Also, ensure you smell pleasant. Stay active, wear a smile, and cultivate a 100% positive attitude. Be kind to everyone and uphold human values. In challenging situations, refrain from reacting; instead observe, listen, and respond. Sometimes, simply giving it time can bring clarity. Allocate time for your family—spouse, children, parents — before extending your focus to relatives and

		friends. Maintain a balanced approach. Keep expectations at zero when dealing with loved ones.
<< No Compromise in this parameter, if this is impacted then all other parameters are going to be impacted >>	<< Unless health issue, this parameter should not be disturbed or impacted. **Remember Work is your Social Identity, be serious >>**	<< Sometimes this parameter gets disturbed due to various reasons, but it's an art... balance it. >>

If you are not following 8:8:8 Rule then there is something wrong with your way of handling the things.

When one segment is affected, it gradually influences the other two segments, creating a web of interconnectedness where data and effects flow between them. If any one segment is impacted, the effects ripple into the other two segments, as illustrated in the diagram below, where you can observe the consequences listed within the intersected area.,

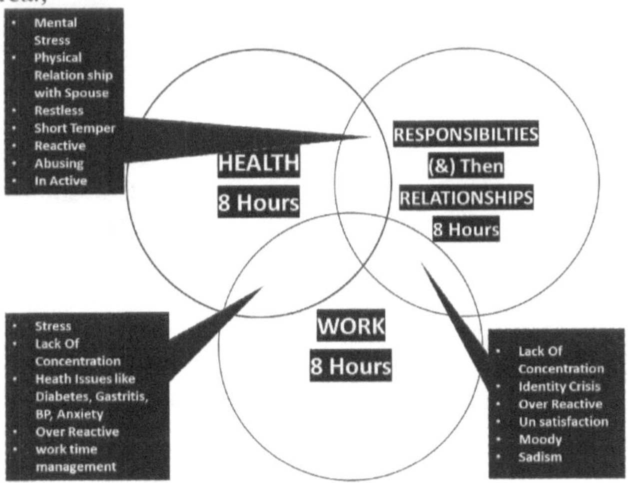

I understand that there may be times when work pressure demands 10-12 hours of daily commitment. However, it's crucial to set limits. Three months, or at most six months, should be the maximum duration to endure such demands.

Beyond six months, you may notice that your health begins to suffer on a smaller scale, leading to disruptions in your relationships with your spouse, children, and others. It's imperative to safeguard your 8:8:8 Rule and ensure that it is not disturbed.

Conduct a Logical Analysis and identify the route cause:
- What are the expectations in this situation?
- Are you learning & progressing to reach the next level?
- Are you overburdened due to incompetence?
- Are you handling more than one job's worth of work?
- Are there any skill gaps that need to be addressed?
- What benefits are you gaining from this situation?
- Are you being compensated fairly?
- Are you shouldering additional responsibilities?
- And so on.

If you ensure that your 8:8:8 rule remains intact, you are likely to find greater satisfaction in your work, as your life's other aspects remain balanced.

"Life is like a journey on the Road – You often use to get Stop signals, Humps, Barricades, Turns, Road Blocks, Sometimes Accidents, Unexpected hurdles. No one can escape from this situation in the journey of life."

> **"Balancing responsibilities and fostering relationships between health and work is indeed an art."**
> **~Raghavendra Prasad MG**

- as shown in the diagram,

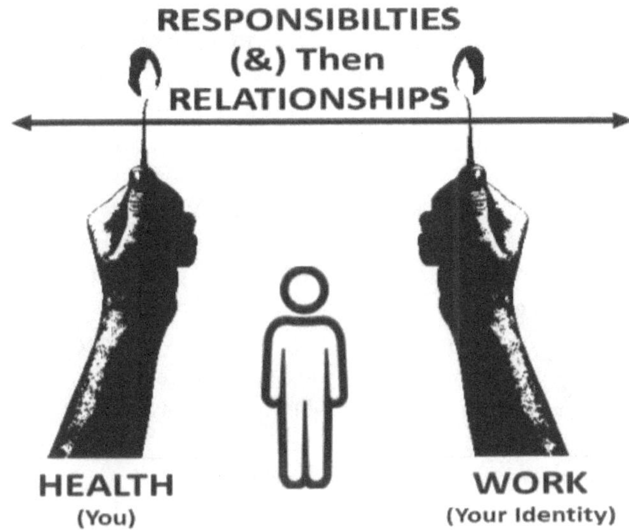

Set a Growth Goal!

Where you aspire to be holds greater importance than your current state. Thus, establish a clear plan for your desired destination and initiate preparations to reach your goal.

For instance, if you aim to prepare a delicious biryani, begin by outlining the steps and gathering the necessary ingredients and execute the preparation step by step.

Ensure that your Growth Goal encompasses the following elements, each supported by accurate information and data, before you embark on your journey:

IMAGINATION | ANALYSIS | PLANNING | PREPARATION | EXECUTION | ITERATION | MONITORING | TRACKING |
Eventually, your efforts will lead to:
RESULTS | CELEBRATION

IMAGINATION:

Imagination stands as the most pivotal factor in achieving your goals. Visualize yourself as if you have already accomplished your goal and revisit this mental image at least 3-4 times a day during your leisure moments.

Why is imagination so effective? The human brain cannot discern the difference between reality and imagination; it responds in the same way to both. When you consistently imagine that you have achieved your goal, you are essentially programming your subconscious mind to accept this imagined scenario as reality. Once your subconscious mind aligns with this vision, it tirelessly works on your behalf, 24/7, and the universe conspires to turn your imagined success into a tangible reality.

God helps him who does his work.

~Mother Theresa

"You must first clearly see a thing in your mind before you can do it."

~Alex Morrison

"Imagination is as important as knowledge"

~Albert Einstein

> **"State of financial freedom can be defined as waking up in the morning with no tasks assigned to you by others, but instead, you hold the responsibility for your own tasks & enjoy your day working towards your passions & goals."**
>
> **~Raghavendra Prasad MG**

Success hinges on having a well-defined goal as your foundation. Here's the roadmap:

- Envision yourself at your ultimate **destination.**
- Lay the mental **groundwork.**

- Progress to comprehensive **preparation**.
- Once preparations are in place, commence **execution**, embracing an **iterative** approach.
- On your journey be **Agile**, **prioritize** achieving even the smallest **milestones**.
- Find joy in each step of the **process**, and persevere.
- Through unwavering **effort**,
- Ultimately, you will undoubtedly reach your ultimate **goal**.

And amidst this journey, remember to pause and celebrate the achievements along the way.

Couple of sayings from the experienced people, proverbs or philosophical teachings in the context of this chapter,

"Follow your passion; it will lead you to your purpose."
~Oprah Winfrey

"Work hard for what you love, and you will find that you have everything you need"

"Passion is the key to success. If you love what you are doing, you will be successful."
~Albert Schweitzer

Personal Notes & Learnings

CHAPTER#7:
Your future is shaped by your words—exercise caution in your speech.

"Positive words can bend your world in your favour."
~Michael Novak

"The words you speak become the house you live in."
~Hafiz

The words you speak, think, and regularly listen to wield a profound impact on your life and shape your future.

You might question, 'How can mere words (human constructs), affect our daily lives?' It's true that words are human constructs, but they are intricately linked to mental images and actions in your mind. For instance:

- The word 'Hit' conjures an image of striking something.
- 'Apple' triggers a mental picture of the fruit itself.

This is how your brain operates. Positive words generate positive mental images, while negative words evoke negative imagery. Your choice of words can significantly influence the direction of your thoughts, emotions, and ultimately, your life.

What you speak, think, and consciously listen to is absorbed by your subconscious mind, which then plays a significant role in manifesting those thoughts into your future. To achieve success, it's crucial to maximize the use of positive words.

For example:

- Instead of 'Fail,' use 'Not Passed' (where you are introducing 'Pass,' a positive word, to your subconscious mind through your conscious thoughts).
- Rather than saying 'half-empty glass of water,' say 'half-filled glass of water' (eliminating the negative connotation).
- Replace 'half door closed' with 'half door opened' (removing the negative aspect).
- Instead of stating 'I don't like Pizza,' say 'I prefer Brugger or Dosa' (substituting the negative 'don't like' with a positive preference).

Incorporating positive language into your conscious thoughts can have a profound impact on your mindset and future outcomes.

Story#1: I know a woman who lives nearby my place. She has a happy family, with a husband who earns well and a lovely child. There were some issues in their husband-and-wife relationship that could have been easily resolved. She always used to say, "I need a loving husband, not just money." Whenever she saw the lives of daily laborers, she would repeatedly express, "I do not have a contented life like them. Why do we need a big house and a fat bank balance?"

Believe it or not, after a few years, her husband lost his factory and their home, and they ended up on the streets. He began working in a local factory and transformed into a loving husband, but they faced a significant financial crisis. Life became tough for her once again. This story serves as a reminder to be careful when thinking, speaking, and listening, as your subconscious mind can influence the events in your life. Whatever you consistently think, speak, and listen to, your subconscious mind which is connected to Universe will work to make it a reality for you.

Story#2: I'd like to share an experiment that took place in Japan, highlighting the importance of listening to positive words and the impact they can have.

In this experiment, two plants were selected, and they were both provided with the same amount of water, sunlight, soil nutrients, and other environmental conditions. The only difference between the two plants was the way they were treated verbally.

One plant received blessings and appreciations, with people saying positive things like, "You are good," "You are so important and vital to the Earth," and using various uplifting words. Meanwhile, the other plant received scolding's and curses, with people using negative words like, "You are bad," "You are useless to the Earth," and other disparaging remarks.

After some time, the results were surprising. The plant that received blessings and appreciations had grown well and appeared healthier. In contrast, the plant that was subjected to scolding's and curses had become weaker and less healthy. This experiment demonstrates how the words we use can have a significant impact on the well-being and growth of living things.

Similarly, in our interactions with children, parents who offer praise and appreciation have a different and more positive impact compared to parents who constantly compare their children to others and criticize them by saying they are not good at certain things. The words and encouragement we provide to our children can shape their self-esteem and overall development.

Would like to share another 2 stories on Sin is in words of mouth.

Story#3: Once upon a time, there was a king who was known for his charitable deeds. On one occasion, he was hosting a lunch for the poor. As the king and the poor citizens enjoyed their meal, an eagle flew high above in the sky, clutching a snake in its talons. Unexpectedly, the snake slipped from the eagle's grip and fell onto one of the people who were partaking in the meal offered by the king. In a state of panic, the snake bit the person, and tragically, the individual succumbed to the snakebite.

Now, the question arose as to who should be held responsible for the person's death:

Eagle: It was argued that the eagle should not be held accountable because it was acting according to its natural instinct for survival by capturing the snake.

Snake: Similarly, it was contended that the snake should not be blamed as it reacted out of fear when its life was in danger, leading it to bite the person.

King: The consensus was that the king could not be held responsible. His intentions were pure in providing food for the impoverished citizens, and he had no control over the unforeseen events that transpired.

However, an old lady had a different perspective. She claimed that if the king hadn't offered the food in the first place, this unfortunate death would never have occurred. She sought to establish the king as the one responsible for the citizen's demise.

This story serves as a reminder of the workings of the universal law. **The old lady, in her attempt to assign blame, ended up bearing the burden of guilt herself**, as the universe reflected the accusations back upon her. It underscores the importance of being mindful of what we say and the consequences our words can have.

Story#4: In the Indian epic Mahabharata, there is a notable character named Shishupal, who happens to be the cousin brother of Sri Krishna. Shishupal met his demise as a punishment for his disrespectful and abusive behaviour towards Sri Krishna. It's worth noting that Shishupal didn't physically harm or cause any destruction; his actions were primarily cantered around using derogatory and offensive language.

This tale from the Mahabharata serves as a powerful reminder that the words we utter can profoundly impact our destiny. Shishupal's fate was sealed by the negative and disrespectful words he directed towards Sri Krishna, ultimately leading to his own downfall. It underscores the importance of being cautious and considerate when we speak, as our words can shape our future and outcomes. It's a valuable lesson in the significance of mindfulness in our communication.

Would like to recall the sayings from the popular Philosophers on Words,

Philosopher Basavanna in his Vachanagalu (Written in Kannada) he says: **"ಮಾತೇ ಮುತ್ತು, ಮಾತೇ ಮೃತ್ಯು" (Maathe Muthu, Maathe Mruthyu)**, The saying **"Speech (Words you speak) is a pearl & Speech (Words you speak) could be death as well"** by the philosopher Basavanna beautifully encapsulates the dual nature of words. It suggests that words can be as precious and valuable as a pearl, but they also have the potential to be as destructive as death when used recklessly or harmfully. This saying serves as a reminder of the power and responsibility that comes with our ability to communicate through speech.

And also, he says: "ಅಯ್ಯ ಎಂದರೆ ಸ್ವರ್ಗ, ಎಲವೋ ಎಂದರೆ ನರಕ" (Ayya Yendare Swarga, Elavo Yendare Naraka) meaning "You can create a heaven around you through your positive words and create a hell through your negative words."

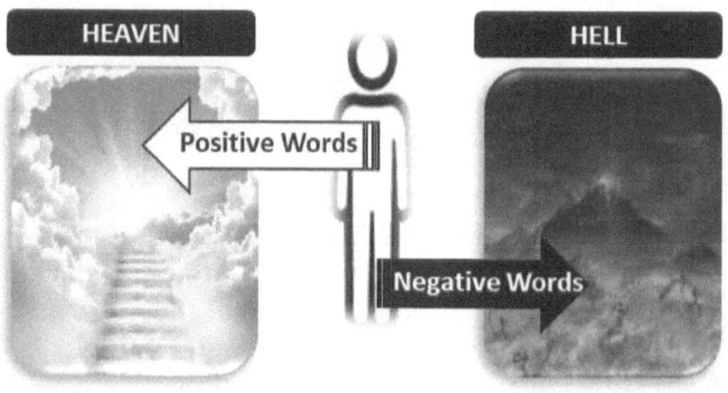

One of my elderly friends always use to say, "It's not just about what you say; it's all about how you say it that matters."

The statement, "If you speak with respect, you are creating a Heaven; if you speak disrespectfully, then you are creating a hell around you," attributed to the philosopher Basavanna, underscores the profound impact of our words and how they shape our environment and relationships. It highlights the idea that speaking with respect and kindness not only enhances our own well-being but also creates a harmonious and positive atmosphere around us, akin to a heavenly state. Conversely, speaking disrespectfully can lead to discord and negativity, akin to a hellish environment. This saying emphasizes the importance of mindful and respectful communication in fostering a better world and interpersonal connections.

There is one saying in Sanskrit, **"द्रक्षम्लना मुखिया जात शंकर चस्मतंगथा सुभाषित रसं द्रष्ट्वा अमृत बेथा देवंगथा"**,

The Sanskrit saying, **"Drakshamlana Mukhi Jaatha, Shankara Chasmatangatha, Subhashitha Rasam Drashtva Amritha Betha Devangatha,"** poetically illustrates the immense power of kind and positive words. It suggests that the impact of good words is so profound that they can transform even the ordinary into something extraordinary.

It means, by listening to the beauty of kind words:
- "Dry grapes shrank its face"
- "Sugar became stone"
- "Amruth left Earth ran away to heaven"

In essence, this saying emphasizes the transformative and uplifting power of positive and kind words, demonstrating how they can enrich our lives and the lives of others.

"The best among you is the one who doesn't harm others with his tongue and hands."

~Extract from Quran

"Do not confuse kind words with being kind. While it's essential to exercise kind words, but exercise being kind with extra caution, as it can be both your strength and your weakness."

~Raghavendra Prasad MG

Couple of sayings from the experienced people, proverbs or philosophical teachings in the context of this chapter,

---

"Kind words can be short and easy to speak, but their echoes are truly endless."

~Mother Teresa

"Speak only if it improves upon the silence."

~Mahatma Gandhi

"Kind words cost nothing."

"One kind word can change someone's entire day."

"Your words are a reflection of your thoughts. Choose them carefully."

"Your words have the power to heal or wound, to uplift or bring down. Choose them wisely."

"The tongue has no bones, but it is strong enough to break a heart. So be careful with your words."

"Kindness is a mark of faith, and whoever has no kindness has no faith."

~Extract from Quran

"The creation of a thousand forests is in one acorn."

~Ralph Waldo Emerson

Personal Notes & Learnings

Personal Notes & Learnings

CHAPTER#8:
Positive Mindset = Heaven (Success) | Negative Mindset = Hell (Failure)

"A positive mind finds opportunity in everything. A negative mind finds fault in everything."

"What you think, you become."
> ~Buddha

"Positivity always wins...Always."
> ~Gary Vaynerchuk

I would like to start this chapter with a story of 2 good friends,

In the bustling city, two inseparable friends, Suresh & Mahesh, embarked on a journey together after completing their degrees. Their shared dream was to secure a job that would lead them toward a brighter future. Every morning, they made a solemn ritual of visiting the local temple to seek divine blessings before venturing out to face the competitive job market.

Suresh faced a multitude of challenges in his life, far beyond the pursuit of employment. With a father absent from his life, he carried the weight of providing for his family, tending to his mother's ailing health, and ensuring his sister's education could continue uninterrupted.

On the other hand, Mahesh, though in need of a job himself, was relatively more self-reliant. While he sought employment, he had fewer pressing responsibilities.

As days turned into weeks and weeks into months, destiny showed its hand. Mahesh's relentless efforts bore fruit, landing him a coveted job that not only secured his own future but also allowed him to support Suresh in meeting his basic needs.

One pleasant afternoon, the two friends found themselves sitting in a serene park, engaged in a heartfelt conversation. Curiosity compelled Suresh to pose a question to Mahesh, "Tell me, my friend, what did you specifically pray for? You've found a stable job and have been a great support to me."

With a warm smile, Mahesh revealed his secret which reflected his selflessness, "In my prayers, I asked for a job not only for myself but also for you, knowing your dire need."

Intrigued, Mahesh returned the inquiry to Suresh, "Dear Friend, what did you pray for?"

Suresh's response radiated his selfishness, "I prayed fervently for my own job but never asked for anything on your behalf. My only wish was for you to secure a job after I did, as you bear lesser burdens and responsibilities.

Story summary:

	To himself	To Others	Result
Mahesh	Positive – Prayed for himself	Positive – Prayed for Suresh	**Positive to self**
Suresh	Positive – Prayed for himself	A kind of Negative – I should get job before Mahesh gets	**Negative to self**

Here is the conclusion,
What you think about others in your context – your subconscious mind, which has a direct connection to the Universe, will ensure that it manifests in your life. This is because the thought originates within you.

See the below table, it will clearly tell you how your Mindset should be, there is **only 2 cases** which can give you clear Positive results.

Case#	About Yourself	About Others	End Result (In Your Context*)
#1	Positive	Positive	Positive (Recommended)
#2	Positive	None	Mostly Positive
#3	None	Positive	Negative
#4	None	None	Negative
#5	Positive	Negative	Negative
#6	Negative	Positive	Negative
#7	Negative	Negative	Negative
#8	None	Negative	Negative

Table #Positive Mindset (You can very much co-relate the above table with Arithmetic & Logical gates)

To achieve a 100% positive result at the end in the broader perspective or long run, follow Case #1 Rule.

OR

Simplify by applying an Arithmetic AND Gate operation, as shown below.

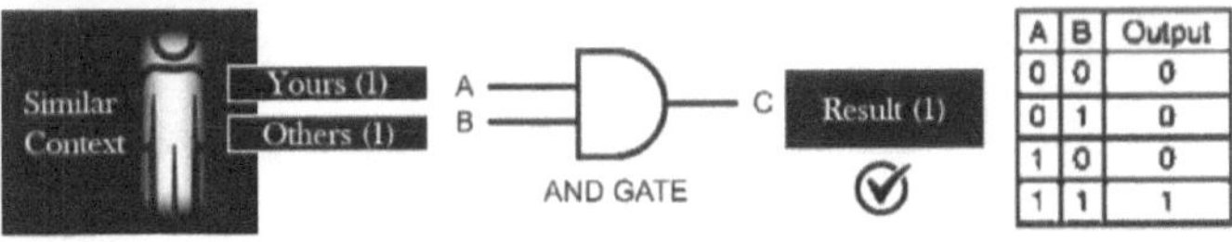

Hence, you should always maintain a positive mindset, whether it's about yourself, others, or any situation you contemplate.

For instance, if you aspire to succeed, focus solely on your own success and not on someone else's failure or defeat. Make a firm commitment that you will approach any setbacks with a positive attitude.

The moment thoughts of failure or defeat enter your mind, your subconscious mind (which is connected to Universe) records them, and it can influence your experiences. Therefore, ensure that no doubts or negative words creep into your mind on your path to success.

When you're in a competition, focus on maintaining a 100% winning attitude. Avoid underestimating or judging any participant, as this negative mindset can hinder your progress. Give your best effort, and remember that whatever results come your way are determined by the laws of the universe. Stay thankful and continue with a positive mindset, as something significant may be waiting for you.

"A positive mindset is halfway to success; the rest is an action."

> **~Raghavendra Prasad MG**

It's quite easy to develop that mindset to think only positive on everything, you must remember the wonderful sayings from Buddha,

> **"Forgive and Forget"**
>> **~Buddha**

Using the above statement for your own benefit,
When you find yourself in a conflict with someone, especially if it's not a mandatory relationship, consider the wisdom of forgiving and forgetting. You might be wondering how this relates to maintaining a positive mindset. Let's draw a comparison: think about a time when you've had pain in your leg. What's your primary focus during that moment? Undoubtedly, it's the pain in your leg. But have you ever considered that there are hundreds of other organs in your body silently performing their functions without your notice? You only become acutely aware of the leg pain because it's causing you discomfort.

Similarly, when you're disturbed by someone's actions or words, it's natural to start dwelling on negative thoughts about that person. However, if you choose to forgive and forget, you free your mind from these negative thoughts. Your mind becomes liberated to focus on your own path to success.

> "In this world, perfection is elusive. What may seem perfect and beneficial today can change over time, altering your perception and end results. Therefore, maintain a positive mindset at every moment in life."

Couple of sayings from the experienced people, proverbs or philosophical teachings in the context of this chapter,

"Your attitude, not your aptitude, will determine your altitude."

~Zig Ziglar

"Once you replace negative thoughts with positive ones, you'll start having positive results."

~Willie Nelson

"Believe in yourself and all that you are. Know that there is something inside you that is greater than any obstacle."

~Christian D. Larson

"Positive thinking is a valuable tool that can help you overcome obstacles, deal with pain, and reach new goals."

~Amy Morin

"Positive thinking is not about expecting the best to happen every time, but accepting that whatever happens is the best for this moment."

~David A. Hunter

Personal Notes & Learnings

CHAPTER#9:
Strong Belief will fetch positive results.!

When things go out of your hand and when you feel all doors are closed then strong Belief works.

"Come to me, all you who are weary and burdened, and I will give you rest."

~Extract from Bible

"The most complete believer in faith is the one with the best character."

~Extract From Quran

"ನಂಬಿ ಕೆಟ್ಟವರಿಲ್ಲ" ("Nambi Kettavarilla")

~Purandara Dasa

a saying in Kannada,
"The one who believes in the Divine will never face any loss."

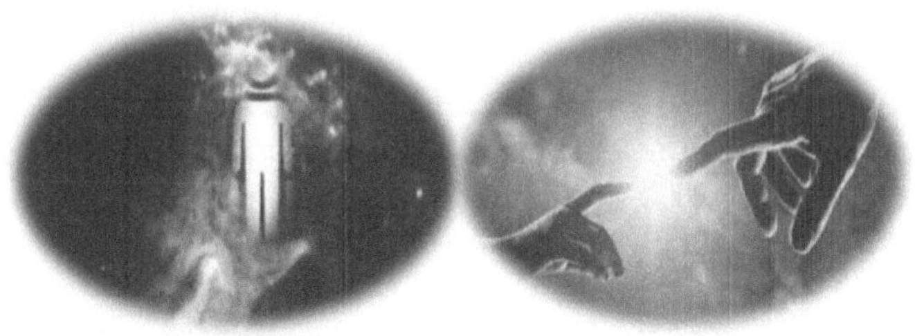

I would like to share 2 real stories on how strong Belief works when things are out of control.

Story#1: There was a radio program happening in New York City where the radio host was inviting listeners to call in and share their wishes or requests that they wanted to convey to God.

During this program, a lady with two children was listening intently. She and her children hadn't had anything to eat for the past two days, and they were desperately hungry.
She decided to call the Radio Jockey and shared her plight, saying, "I and my children haven't had anything to eat for the last two days. I want to request God to send us some food so we can survive."
Upon hearing the lady's plea, the radio jockey responded with comforting words, "God is listening to you; have faith. He will send you the food you need. Please tell me your address." The lady provided her address, and the call ended.

At the same time, there was a man who didn't believe in God, listening to the same program. He instructed his assistant to gather some food and deliver it to the lady who had just spoken on the radio. He told his assistant to inform her that the food was sent by the Devil. He wanted to test whether she would accept and eat the food sent by a devil not by the god.

As per his master's instructions, the assistant handed over the food to the lady, who received it with happiness. She sat down with her children and began eating the food. The assistant was puzzled by her lack of curiosity about the sender and asked, "Aren't you curious? Don't you want to know who sent this food for you?"

With a warm smile, the lady replied, "If God commands it, even the Devil can send food."

And that's where our story ends. It teaches us that when life seems devoid of options and all doors appear closed, the universe often finds a way to continue our journey. Ultimately, having a strong belief can yield remarkable results.

Story#2: Once upon a time, there was an Orthopaedic Surgeon named Dr. Ahmed, known far and wide for his expertise in handling complicated surgeries. Despite his success, he often found himself pondering the purpose of life. Questions like "Why am I here? What am I doing? Why do I do what I do?" lingered in his mind.

One day, he received an invitation to an award ceremony celebrating his achievements. Excited, he planned a long 12-hour car journey to attend the event.

However, as he embarked on his journey, fate had other plans. Heavy rain and strong winds caused a massive tree to fall, blocking the road. The power went out, leaving Dr. Ahmed stranded in the darkness. With no way to move forward, he decided himself to spending the night there.

Desperate, he walked a little and stumbled upon a small house dimly lit. Knocking on the door, an elderly lady welcomed him inside. Dr. Ahmed explained his situation, saying, "I was passing through when I got stuck due to a fallen tree on the road. I need a place to stay for the night and plan to continue my journey tomorrow."

The kind old lady agreed, saying, "Please come inside, sir. Freshen up, and I'll prepare something for you. You can rest here tonight and leave in the morning."

Dr. Ahmed freshened up and had dinner, but he couldn't sleep. He worried about missing the award ceremony the next day.

At 4 AM, he noticed the old lady standing before a statue of Jesus Christ, deep in prayer. Beside her sat a young boy of about 5 or 6 years old. Curiosity got the better of him, and he approached the door quietly to observe.

The old lady prayed fervently, "Oh God, I believe in you, and my life is coming to an end. My final wish is to see my grandson walk independently. I've heard of a famous doctor named Dr. Ahmed who lives far from here. Please guide us to him and help us find a solution."

Dr. Ahmed was deeply moved and suddenly realized the purpose of his life. Sometimes, we are in certain positions or places because of someone's wishes, needs, etc whether directly or indirectly. He understood that he needed to act on this calling.
Filled with happiness and determination, he took the young boy to his hometown and performed a successful surgery on his legs. The boy's life was forever changed, and he went on to lead a long, fulfilling life.

This story teaches us that when we feel trapped with no options left, strong belief and selflessness purpose can lead us to unexpected and meaningful outcomes. It reminds us that even in the darkest of times, there is always a glimmer of hope.

"All of us are connected to a vast support system (part of connected universe) that operates seamlessly 24/7 to make our belief systems possible."

~Raghavendra Prasad MG

Here is a typical example,
Imagine you want to visit a holy place, whether it's a temple, church, or mosque, tomorrow. When you wake up in the morning, take a moment to see how the vast support system seamlessly works to manifest your belief system.
As you wake up:
1. The universe is serene and unchanging.
2. The Milky Way galaxy is constantly in motion
3. The sun rises precisely as expected and providing required amount of light and heat to Earth.

4. Earth continues its steady rotation at a calculated pace.
5. The moon carries out its celestial duties.
6. As usual Trees and plants are supplying Oxygen to all living beings on earth
7. You wake up in good health, with all the complex organs in your body functioning as they should.
8. Your family members are also in good health and share a positive mindset.
9. All relatives / friends are all well at place
10. Electricity flows, ensuring your appliances work, whether it's your heater or yesterday's sunshine heating your solar tank water.
11. Clean, fresh water is delivered to your home.
12. Milk and vegetables arrive, offering nourishment.
13. Your home is stocked with provisions.
14. Your car is in optimal condition, with a tank filled with Gasoline.
15. You have flowers, oil, and incense sticks ready for your offerings to God.
16. The road is constructed & well maintained by the Public Works Dept.
17. Municipal Council ensured road is kept clean
18. The road is clear and peaceful as you drive without obstacles.
19. Arriving at the holy place, you find ample parking for your car.
20. The temple priest has already prepared and cleaned the surroundings, and the deity is beautifully adorned with flowers and lit lamps.
21. You stand in front of the deity, offering your prayers for a few precious moments.
22. Safely, you return home.

This narrative illustrates how a multitude of systems and individuals work harmoniously to make your belief system a reality. It's a reminder of the many people and processes we should be thankful for, as they play a crucial role in facilitating our spiritual practices & beliefs in this case.

Now, you can appreciate how many people you should be thankful for, as they contribute to making your belief system a reality.

"Similarly, consider the support systems that surround your primary support system. It's a complex web of dependencies that can be more intricate than you might imagine.

To broaden your perspective, apply this concept to other systems, such as healthcare, education, law enforcement, transportation, and more. In each of these domains, there exists an extensive support network working diligently to meet your needs and assist you in achieving your goals."

Stay blessed and show gratitude, be grateful for everything you have today, whether you're aware of it or not.

Couple of sayings from the experienced people, proverbs or philosophical teachings in the context of this chapter,

"Your beliefs become your thoughts, your thoughts become your words, your words become your actions, your actions become your habits, your habits become your values, your values become your destiny."
~Mahatma Gandhi

"Believe you can and you're halfway there."
~Theodore Roosevelt

"The thing always happens that you really believe in, and the belief in a thing makes it happen.   "
~Frank Lloyd Wright

"Belief in oneself is one of the most important bricks in building any successful venture."
~Lydia M. Child

"The biggest difference I've noticed between successful people and unsuccessful people isn't intelligence or opportunity or resources. It's the belief that they can make their goals happen."
~James Clear

"To be a champ, you have to believe in yourself when nobody else will."
~Sugar Ray Robinson

"Believe in your infinite potential. Your only limitations are those you set upon yourself."
~Roy T. Bennett

"He who has no faith in himself can never have faith in God."
~Guru Nanak

Personal Notes & Learnings

CHAPTER#10:
Picture your Future to change your future!

Dreams are extremely important. You can't do it unless you imagine it.

~George Lucas

"The world is a drama, staged in a dream."

~Guru Nanak

What you think is what you see in your surroundings, and what you see is what you get. You might not believe it just by reading this sentence, but I'll help you understand how your brain and mind work.

Imagine you have long hair, and you've been thinking about getting a haircut. As you walk down the street, you start noticing barber shops. This is your brain's way of playing a game with you. Your subconscious thought about getting a haircut makes you more aware of barber shops, and so you see them more often.

Likewise, the same principle applies in various situations:

- When you're feeling sick, you tend to notice clinics and hospitals.
- If you need medicine, you'll spot a series of medical shops.
- Elderly people often come across parks and temples.
- Parents with children often find themselves noticing play homes and schools.
- Young men are more likely to notice young and attractive women.
- If you're desperately searching for a restroom, you'll suddenly spot public toilets on the road, and nothing else.
- The list goes on.

You may have experienced these situations in your own life, where your brain and mind help you find what you've been thinking about or needing.

It's similar to a Google search:
what you input determines the relevance of the results you receive.

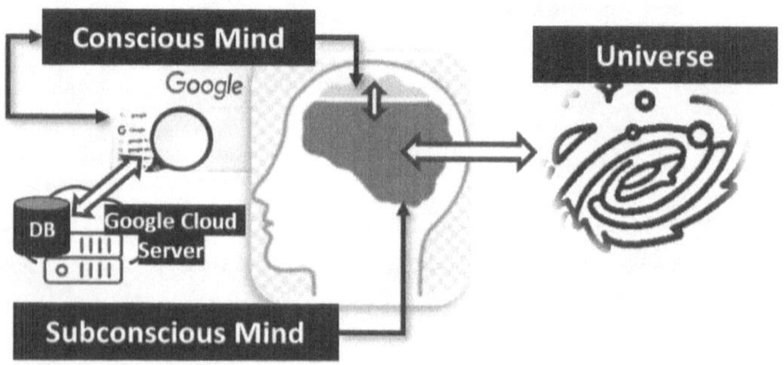

In this chapter, you will gain insights into how you can program your brain to recognize the path to success and guide you towards achieving it.

Your brain does not differentiate between imagination and reality.

For example,

#Action	When we experience or imagine a win or Confident	When we experience or imagine a failure or under stress
The brain instructs your body to release specific hormones in various states of your mind.	**Hormones > Brain Chemical Reaction or response** **Endorphins**: Released through activities such as exercising, listening to music, watching movies, and laughing. **Dopamine**: Released when enjoying food, achieving goals, completing tasks, and engaging in self-care activities. **Serotonin**: Boosted by sun exposure, mindfulness, spending time in nature, and meditation.	**Hormones > Brain Chemical Reaction or response** **Cortisol**: Maintaining the right balance of cortisol is crucial for our health, as producing too much or too little cortisol can lead to health issues. **Short-Term Effects**: Stress , Increased sugar levels, Irritability, Headaches **Long-Term Effects**: Weight gain, Anxiety, Depression, Digestive problems, Mental tension, Muscle pain, Heart disease, Heart attack, High blood pressure and stroke

	Oxytocin: Generated through socializing, physical touch, petting animals, helping others, and giving to others.	Sleep problems, Memory and concentration impairments.
Mind Reaction	Mind will encourage you to safely engage in a task once more.	Mind ensures feelings of acceptance and safety, do not let you to do anything.
Result	Confidence Joyful Happiness Grateful Fortunate Optimism Feeling supported by the world	Insecurity Lack of confidence Embarrassment Anxiety Misfortune Unluckiness Anger Sadness Shame Pessimism Feeling like the world is against you

> "Consider yourself the storywriter, producer, director, cinematographer, and an Actor in the movie of your life. Why settle for a supporting or negative role when you can play the majestic lead role of success?"
> ~ Raghavendra Prasad MG

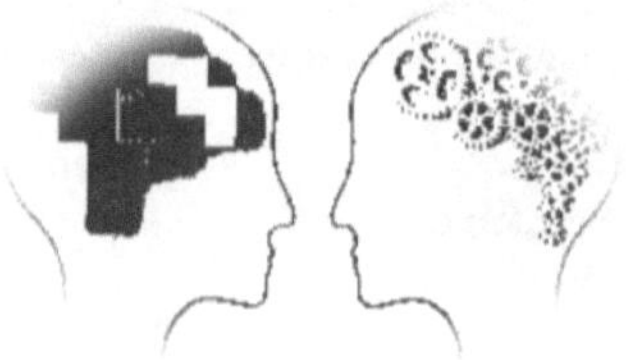

If you aspire to achieve success, cultivate a powerful mindset – craft a script for your own success story and begin believing in it as if it has already unfolded in your life.

"All ordinary individuals transform into the extraordinary because they believe in their potential for success."

Take, for example, the journey of an ordinary bus conductor who became a superstar like Rajinikanth. His vision and mindset were the initial steps toward his success, followed by relentless hard work.

Never underestimate the power of your mind. Remember, the universe and the world are mere reflections of your thoughts.

It's your birthright, and you're here to achieve success and lead a healthy, prosperous, and abundant life.

Thoughts/ Goals	**Thoughts and goals come and go constantly. On any given day, an average human being experiences over ~60,000 thoughts passing through their mind. Out of these:** - Approximately 50% to 75% are focused on the past, - Around 25% to 50% revolve around the future, - Only about 5% to 10% of our thoughts are grounded in the present moment. **Now, consider how most individuals spend their lives, with such a small fraction of their thoughts rooted in the present**
Conscious Mind	- Strong thoughts can be controlled by willpower. - A 'can do' attitude is essential. - Confidence plays a significant role. - Success demands hard work.

Sub Conscious Mind	- By shifting thoughts to the subconscious mind, you gain the support of the Universe. - Stress and pressure to achieve your goals diminish. - **Your subconscious mind works tirelessly, 24/7, to make your goals a reality – remember it's not logical, it won't understand which is good or bad for you.** - You'll experience a sense of miracles unfolding as you work towards your goals. - Achieving your goals becomes a certainty, with a 100% success rate. - Your subconscious mind expertly manages risks, mitigations, and contingencies.

How to test if your subconscious mind is responding to you?

Try this simple experiment: While sleeping at night, set an intention to wake up at exactly 5 AM without using an alarm clock. Just keep a watch or clock beside you. When you wake up, check the time. If it's around 5 AM (+/- 10 minutes), it suggests that you have successfully cultivated a habit of communicating with your subconscious mind. If not, consider dedicating about 30 minutes each day to talking & reflecting to yourself. Over a period of time, your subconscious mind will become more responsive, aligned with your intentions/ thoughts and work for you tirelessly 24/7 to make your thoughts in to reality.

How to Imprint Your Thoughts/ Goals on Your Subconscious Mind:

- Make positive thinking about your goals a daily habit.
- By doing so, you're transmitting information from your conscious mind to your subconscious.
- Through your habit, you'll begin to visualize and feel success, and the Universe will collaborate to help you manifest it.
- Ultimately, success becomes yours.

Practicing these principles requires dedication and a shift in Mindset or Thought Process, which you will learn more about in the upcoming chapters.

"I hope you've heard of **Prompt Engineering** in AI/GenAI, which is essentially about providing precise input with a clear context on what you need to the machine to generate intelligent human-like responses. Similarly, in life, it's important to know what you want and why. This way, you can communicate your goals clearly to your subconscious mind, enabling it to work effectively in making those goals a reality."

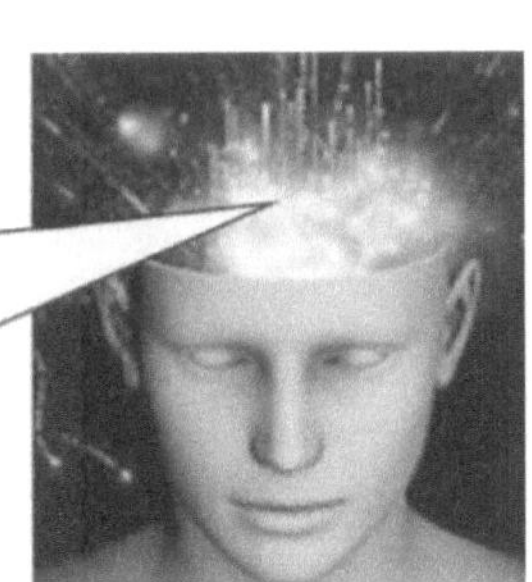

Couple of sayings from the experienced people, proverbs or philosophical teachings in the context of this chapter,

"यद्भवं तद् भवति" ("Yadbhavam tad bhavati") - is a Sanskrit phrase that means **"You become what you think."** Written Thousands of years ago.

In Vishnu Sahasra Nama written Thousands of Years ago, – it says

"कायेन वाचा मन-सेन्द्रियेर्वा | बुद्धात्मा-नावा प्रकृते-स्वभा-वात्" ("Kayena vaachha mana-sendhriyerva | Buddhyatma-naavaa prakrutey-svabha-vaat")
Meaning, by body, speech, mind, intellect, and senses, | through the Soul, inner self, and is by one's nature.

"What you think you become.
What you feel you attract.
What you imagine you create."
~Buddha

"The future belongs to those who believe in the beauty of their dreams."
~Eleanor Roosevelt

"Dreams can become a reality when we possess a vision, a plan, and the courage to chase after it relentlessly."
~ Walt Disney

"Dreams are the touchstones of our character."
~Henry David

"The biggest adventure you can take is to live the life of your dreams."
~Oprah Winfrey

Personal Notes & Learnings

Personal Notes & Learnings

CHAPTER#11:
Live in the Present

"Yesterday is history, tomorrow is a mystery, today is a gift, which is why we call it the present."

~Bil Keane

"We suffer more afraid than actually hurt"
"We suffer more often in imagination than in reality"

~Seneca

Let me start this chapter with an example. Imagine you are traveling on a ship, and halfway through your journey, you discover a leak in the ship, causing water to enter. You have 3 options for how to react or respond to the situation:

1. **Root Cause Analysis** -RCA (Non-Actionable)
2. Taking **Immediate Action** (Actionable)
3. **Timing** of Past or Future Actions (Non-Actionable)

⏱ PAST Non-Actionable	⦾ PRESENT Actionable	↻ FUTURE Non-Actionable
Route Cause Analysis – This involves investigating the manufacturing mistake, configurations, quality issues, and steering problems that led to the leak. It focuses on understanding the underlying causes of the issue.	**Immediate Action** – This entails taking swift action to address the most pressing concern, in this case, patching the hole in the ship. It prioritizes resolving the issue at hand without delay.	**Timing Considerations (Past or Future)** – This involves reflecting on decisions made in the past and how they might have affected the current situation, such as leaving earlier to reach the destination sooner or having the captain drive the ship faster.
No Outcome ✗	**Outcome** ✓	**No Outcome** ✗

PAST	PRESENT	FUTURE
Memory **(Non-Actionable)** **IMAGINATION** **(No Action Can Be Taken at Present)**	**Now ()** **(ACTIONABLE)** **HAPPENNING** **(True by 100%) Useful, Action can be taken at present.**	**Anticipation/Pre diction (Future) (NON-ACTIONABLE) << IMAGINATION >> (Might not be True) You can take Precautionary measures, but No Action can be taken at present.**
Regrets Guilt Complaints Criticizing Rejecting Revenges Grudges Challenges Blame Expectations Perceptions Feedback Judgments Hatred Resistance Lack of Practical Execution, And more	Practical Execution Observing and Experiencing the Surroundings Awareness of Goals and Objectives Taking Iterative Steps Toward Success or Goal Achievement Planning Retrospection Mitigations and Contingencies Task Completions Finding Purpose in Life Enjoying Short-Term Pleasures (with limits)	Wants Desires Responsibilities Expectations The need to prove oneself Earning Imaginations Curses Blames Perceptions Lack of Practical Execution And more

What you should to Carry Forward from the Past:
Experiences
Lessons
Learnings
Positive Outcomes
Effective Forecasting

> ### What you should Focus on through Future Thinking:
> Vision
> A clear blueprint of your desired
> achievements or aspirations
> Execution plans
> Estimations
> Milestones
> What comes next
> ### The impact of present actions on future results

Remember that when you are awake, strive to live in the present at least 90% of the time. Reflect on the past and present, focusing only on actionable items that contribute to your goals. Do this either when you wake up or just before bedtime.

Living in the present doesn't mean indulging in short-lived pleasures like excessive screen time, overindulgence in food, casual sex, alcohol, drugs, etc. It also doesn't involve attempting to change someone, as that is beyond your control. Be mindful and exercise restraint, understanding the purpose of life and the goals you aim to achieve.

Your current state, today's present, is a result of the decisions you made yesterday in the past. Your future, tomorrow's reality, hinges on the choices you make today. (Extract from Chapter #6)
As I've mentioned before, the universe and the world are reflections of your own being. Nothing else. You determine your future by living in the present.

Remember, today's present will become tomorrow's past, but by living in the present, you can shape your future according to your desires.

Living in the present will bring efficiency:
If you've set a goal to achieve something in the next 3 months, as an example, let's consider dividing the overall goal into 5 parts. Plan and execute in stages from Stage #1 to #5, Assume efficiency measuring scale from 0 to 1.

Below is a table that illustrates the ideal way of execution. By giving your 100% effort at each stage, you can reach your goal with 100% efficiency.

	Plan	Step#1	Step#2	Step#3	Step#4	Step#5	Final Result %
Ideal	1	1	1	1	1	1	
Efficiency	1	1	1	1	1	1	100%

Below is the table. In reality, assume you are giving your best between 70% to 90%. The overall result in achieving the goal will be at a 68% efficiency.

	Plan	Step#1	Step#2	Step#3	Step#4	Step#5	Final Result %
Actual	0.8	0.9	0.8	0.7	0.8	0.9	
Efficiency	0.8	0.72	0.72	0.56	0.56	0.72	68%

"Therefore, giving your best through actions by living in the present is highly necessary to achieve your goals."

Develop Objective Mindset:

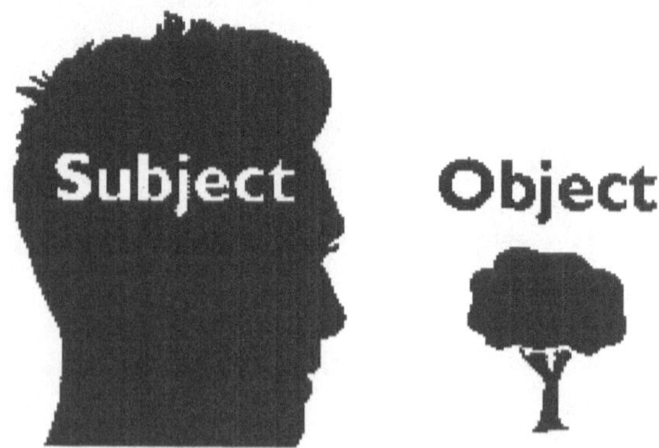

Develop | Promote Objective Thinking & Conversations	Avoid Subjective Thinking & Conversations
Objective refers to: (Reality) Facts Truth Actual Data Evidence Proof	**Subjective refers to: (Personal Point of View or Perception)** Opinions Feelings Emotions Personal Benefit Feedback Thoughts Expectations Desires Rumors Gossips Perceptions You will tend to hear these worlds frequently in subjective discussions: I, me, my, I think, as per me, I am, you are, He is, they are, etc.
Example, Sun raises in the East and set at West.	Example, I like summer, and hot Sun.
Always promote and support objective-based conversations and discussions. They provide realistic information, trends, and data that remain consistent and unbiased. Unlike subjective information,	Avoid subjective-based conversations and discussions, as they tend to be filled with personal opinions and points of view that often favor the speaker's interests or areas of bias. Engaging in such conversations increases

which can be influenced by personal perspectives, objective data is reliable and keeps you from being misled.	the likelihood of being misled and it may dilute your objective thoughts.
In grammar, objectivity can also refer to the 'object' in a sentence, which is typically a noun that the subject of the sentence acts upon	In grammar, subjectivity refers to any qualities that pertain to the subject of a sentence

Both object and subject are closely related. For instance, the 'Sun' is an object, but your thoughts about the 'Sun' and its effects are subjective. Therefore, when engaging in conversations, it's advisable to approach the discussion with objective information first. Subjective viewpoints, being personal in nature, may not align with others' perspectives. It's often better to avoid introducing subjective information, actively listen to others, and synthesize objective information before arriving at a final conclusion.

> "See the world & around 'As It Is' (object) not based on your assumptions or perceptions (subject)"
> ~Raghavendra Prasad MG

The subject plays a major role in life, but it's important to be cautious.

What we see often becomes our perception (subjective), and what we hear is an opinion (subjective). The objective element is missing here. Therefore, it's essential to consistently evaluate perceptions and opinions by cultivating objective thinking.

Story on the same line: Once upon a time, there was a king who lived a life of luxury and was addicted to vices like alcohol consumption and gambling. His addiction eventually led to the loss of his kingdom, and he was banished to the wilderness. As the sun began to set, he desperately searched for shelter for the night.

In the distance, he spotted a humble hut. Weary and dejected, he approached the hut and found a saint meditating inside. The king stood before the meditating saint for quite some time until the saint opened his eyes and learned of the king's tragic tale.

Moved by the king's plight, the saint offered him a place to spend the night and some fruits and vegetables to eat. However, the king, accustomed to a life of extravagance, declined and requested a more luxurious meal. The saint, treating the king as a guest of honor, agreed to fulfill his request. With a chant of a mantra, a sumptuous feast appeared before the king, who relished every bite and was overjoyed.

When it was time to sleep, the saint directed the king to a simple mat on the floor in another hut. Again, the king protested, claiming he was accustomed to sleeping on a soft mattress with female attendants fanning him. The saint, undeterred, used his powers to provide the king with a lavish setup.

Satisfied, the king drifted into a deep sleep. However, when he awoke in the morning, all the luxury had vanished, and he found himself back on the floor mat. The king was astonished by the saint's powers and yearned to attain them.

Looking at the saint, who was once again deep in meditation, the king waited patiently. Eventually, the saint opened his eyes and questioned why the king had not left as he was supposed to that morning.

The king expressed his desire to acquire the saint's powers to regain his kingdom and live a life of prosperity. The saint cautioned that it would require immense dedication, concentration, and hard work. Undeterred, the king agreed to anything and eagerly awaited the saint's guidance.

The saint instructed the king to wake up at 4 AM, take a cold-water bath, and chant mantras continuously for six hours each day, maintaining a positive mindset while consuming only fruits and vegetables for the next six months. The king diligently followed the instructions, but after six months, there was no discernible progress.

Frustrated, the king returned to the saint, who advised him to repeat the process while standing on one leg during the chants. The king complied but still failed to achieve any results. He was disheartened and approached the saint with a knife, intending to end his life.

The saint, however, spoke honestly, acknowledging that the mantras had worked for him but not for the king. He explained that the king lacked concentration and understanding of the mantras' true purpose. The saint emphasized that the king had merely followed instructions without comprehending the deeper meaning, leading to his failure.

The moral of this story is that objective thinking is crucial when striving to achieve one's goals. Subjective thinking, driven by personal desires and expectations, often leads to disappointment and failure. To attain true success, it is essential to focus on the objective, understanding its purpose and working diligently towards it.

Would like to co-relate real time examples with the above story,

Example#1, Let's assume someone has a Vitamin D3 Deficiency. now he wanted to get out of it. if Vitamin D3 deficiency is solved he will come out of Muscle pain, uneasiness, etc.

How Objective and Subjective Thinking plays a role in solving the problem is illustrated below,

Objective Thinking:
Problem Identification: Identify Vitamin D3 deficiency as the root cause of muscle pain and uneasiness.

Research and Information Gathering: Gather information on the importance of Vitamin D3, its sources, and its effects on health.

Consult a Healthcare Professional: Seek advice from a healthcare provider for an accurate diagnosis and recommended treatment.

Treatment Plan: Develop a treatment plan based on the healthcare provider's recommendations, including the use of medication if necessary.

Sunlight Exposure: Spend time in the sun as advised by the healthcare provider to naturally boost Vitamin D3 levels.

Dietary Changes: Adjust the diet to include foods rich in Vitamin D3, such as fatty fish, fortified dairy products, and supplements as prescribed.

Monitoring: Regularly check Vitamin D3 levels through blood tests to track progress.

Subjective Thinking:
Physical: Commit to spending time outdoors in the sunlight as recommended by the healthcare provider.
Mental: Maintain a positive mindset, believing that the Vitamin D3 deficiency can be cured and focusing on overall health.

Final Outcome:
The final outcome is the successful cure of Vitamin D3 deficiency through a combination of medical treatment, sunlight exposure, dietary changes, and a positive mindset. This plan provides a structured approach to addressing the issue and helps ensure that all necessary steps are taken to alleviate the symptoms associated with Vitamin D3 deficiency.

Example#2: Let me give you another example, of Objective & Subjective Thinking
Assume that you want to Drink Sugar Cane Juice.
Subjective thinking involves the desire or imagination of the end result, which, in this case, is drinking sugar cane juice with an enjoyment.

Objective thinking, on the other hand, focuses on the practical steps and components required to achieve that end result, such as the need for sugar cane and a crushing machine to extract the juice.

This is how you need to make efficient use of Objective & Subjective ways of thinking.

Living in the present enables you to concentrate on the current moment and empowers you to act based on objective thinking. The subjective aspects will naturally align with this approach, and you can personally experience them as part of the end result.

Before concluding this chapter, let's draw a correlation between the concept of Objective Thinking with the Object-Oriented Programming (OOPs) concepts used in the Software Programming languages like C++ or Java.

In OOPs, a 'Class' can be seen as a 'Fact.' When you create an 'Instance' of a Class, it becomes an 'Object.' Just as an Object can undergo various states and behaviors based on the attributes or variables/values you set; your perception can also change over time concerning a particular Object.

Therefore, it's always recommended to provide or assign the right attributes and variables/ values to achieve success in positive way – as clearly depicted in the diagram,

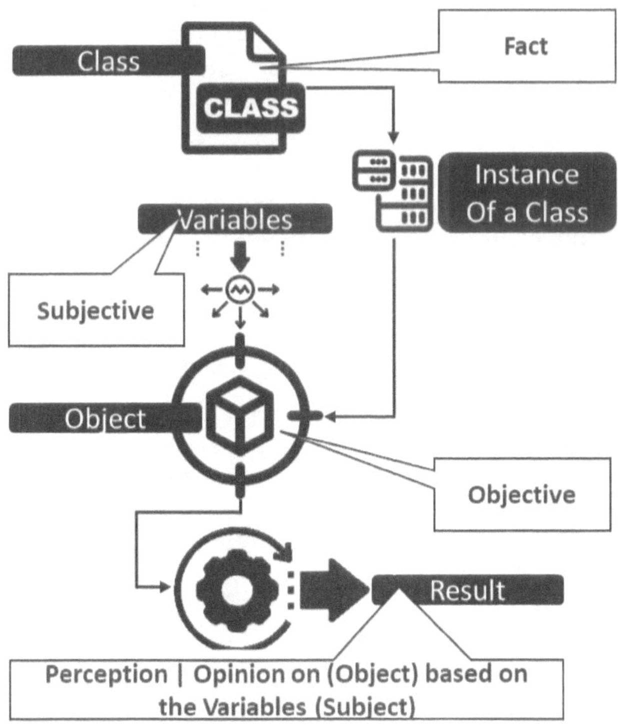

Couple of sayings from the experienced people, proverbs or philosophical teachings in the context of this chapter,

"Your present situation is the result of your own thoughts and decisions made in the past."

~Sri Krishna

"Realise deeply that the present moment is all you ever have."

~Eckhart Tolle

"Life is available only in the present moment."
~Thich Nhat Hanh

"The secret of health for both mind and body is not to mourn for the past, not to worry about the future, or not to anticipate troubles, but to live in the present moment wisely and earnestly."

~Buddha

"Do not dwell in the past, do not dream of the future, concentrate the mind on the present moment."
~Buddha

"The best way to predict your future is to create it."
~Abraham Lincoln

"Forever is composed of now's."
~Emily Dickinson

"The present moment is filled with joy and happiness. If you are attentive, you will see it."
~Thich Nhat Hanh

"You must live in the present, launch yourself on every wave, find your eternity in each moment."

~Henry David Thoreau

"The ability to be in the present moment is a major component of mental wellness."

~Abraham Maslow

"Life is now. There was never a time when your life was not now, nor will there ever be."

~Eckhart Tolle

"The past is behind, learn from it. The future is ahead, prepare for it. The present is here, live it."

~Thomas S. Monson

Personal Notes & Learnings

CHAPTER#12:
Keep your Weakness & Personal Matters Private.

"The biggest guru-mantra is: never share your secrets with anybody. It will destroy you."

~Chanakya

"Guard your personal matters and weaknesses like precious treasures, for sharing them may lead to unforeseen consequences."

"Privacy is not about something to hide. Privacy is about something to protect."

~Glenn Greenwald

Here are the few places you might tend to freely leak or talk about your weakness where they take advantages out of it,

- Friends
- Relatives
- Astrologers
- Priests/ Imam/ bishop
- Social Media
- So, on...

Astrologers:
When you visit an astrologer, it's typically because you have certain expectations for your life or are facing a problem you'd like to resolve. While an astrologer may not fully understand the exact nature of your problem, they possess the intelligence to detect your vulnerabilities or concerns. Here are some common ways astrologers provide solutions:

Planetary Positions: Astrologers may examine your astrological chart and conclude that all planetary positions are favourable except for one specific planet, which they believe is causing your current challenges. They may suggest remedies to balance or appease this planet.

Black Magic Claims: Some astrologers may suggest that your problems are a result of black magic or negative energies directed towards you. In such cases, they offer solutions that typically involve prayers, rituals, or offerings to counteract these negative influences.

Offerings and Charity: Astrologers often recommend specific offerings, prayers, or acts of charity to appease the planets and seek their Favor. This might include donations to charitable causes, feeding animals, or helping the less fortunate in some way. These recommendations are typically accompanied by a fee for the astrologer's services.

Gemstone Recommendations: Astrologers who specialize in gemstone predictions may suggest wearing a particular gemstone to harness its positive energy or counteract negative influences. The choice of gemstone may vary based on your astrological profile connected to your financial situation.

Mantra Chanting: Some astrologers advocate the chanting of specific mantras for a designated period (e.g., 15, 21, or 108 days) to address specific issues. The repetition of these sacred sounds is believed to have a positive impact on your life and can be seen as a form of spiritual practice.

Poojas and Rituals: In cases where astrologers perceive your weaknesses or challenges as particularly severe, they may propose conducting elaborate rituals or poojas on your behalf. These rituals can be quite expensive and are intended to invoke divine intervention to resolve your problems.

Astrologer is doing his job of survival, whatever problem you take to him whether it may be related to Health, education, financial, job or personal relationships – his solution will be around his business centric – which will be within the above listed items.

It's essential to exercise caution and discretion when consulting astrologers. While some may genuinely offer guidance and support, most of them may take advantage of your vulnerabilities for their financial gain. Always consider seeking multiple opinions and do your research before making any significant decisions based on astrological advice. Remember that your actions and choices play a significant role in shaping your destiny, and no one can guarantee specific outcomes through astrological remedies.

Would like to share one story on this front,

Once upon a time in a quiet village, a Saint arrived carrying three mysterious stones in his bag. He proclaimed that these three stones possessed the power to work miracles. Intrigued by his claim, the villagers gathered outside the village, eager to witness this extraordinary feat.

The Saint placed all three stones into a large vessel and lit a fire beneath it. He then requested a villager to fetch some water, which he poured into the vessel. As the water began to boil, anticipation filled the air. The villagers watched in fascination, wondering what would happen next.

The Saint, however, informed them that some more time was needed to complete the process. He asked for a small quantity of rice and later requested some vegetables. Finally, he declared, "It is done," and proceeded to distribute freshly cooked food to all the villagers.

If you closely observe, saint did not engage in obtaining the items needed for cooking apart from 3 Stones (which is actually of no use in reality). Instead, these items, such as wood for fire, water, vegetables, and rice, are unknowingly supplied by people.

The moral of this story is clear: no one possesses the power to work magic in your life except yourself. True transformations and achievements come through unwavering dedication, discipline, and the cultivation of positive habits.

Numerology:

People often concern themselves with numbers, believing that certain numbers are good for them while others are not. Changing one's name according to numerology or attributing bad luck to one's date of birth often hinges on coincidences rather than concrete evidence. These beliefs are often indicative of a weak mindset. This book delves into the concept of achieving positive results through the right thought process.

Allow me to share a personal experience from when I was in my early twenties. Someone once told me that the numbers 7 and 4 seemed to play a significant role in various aspects of my life. These numbers appeared in my siblings' birthdates, my spouse's birthdate, examination registration numbers, vehicle registration numbers, and more. Surprisingly, I started noticing the presence of either 7 or 4 almost everywhere I went. It became a habit to check for these numbers on train/ flight tickets, the seats I occupied, registration numbers, door numbers, employment IDs, and so on.

However, something interesting happened just a few months ago when I began practicing the science of mathematical methods to shape my own future. Whether you believe it or not, the numbers 7 and 4 mysteriously disappeared from my life. This change extended to property numbers, tickets, vehicle registration numbers, and other aspects.

This experience taught me a valuable lesson: our thoughts have a powerful influence on our reality. What you think, you see; what you see, you get. You'll find more insights on this in other chapters.

Priests/ Imam/ bishop:

As a secular individual, I'm neither advocating nor opposing any particular religion in this discussion. When you visit a temple, mosque, or church, it's generally expected to offer your prayers and offerings and then depart.

However, if you engage in conversations with the priest, imam, or bishop who conducts rituals on behalf of their respective deities, assuming they are closer to God, there's a risk that they may exploit any vulnerabilities they perceive in your beliefs. They may lead you into costly rituals and encourage offerings to themselves in the name of God.

In the case of astrologers and priests, they often work on your subconscious mind, instilling a sense of trust by assuring you that your problems will be solved or your desires fulfilled if you follow their guidance. The challenge here is that if you choose not to follow their advice, you might start believing that your problems persist or your wishes remain unfulfilled due to your inaction.

Conversely, if you faithfully follow the recommendations of astrologers or priests and assume that your desires have been fulfilled as you wished, you may become a loyal and recurrent customer for that particular astrologer, priest, or holy place.

Similarly, those who have experienced positive outcomes through such practices tend to return to these sources whenever they encounter problems or have new needs.

In cases where the recommended actions do not yield the desired results, it becomes challenging to seek any guarantees. In such instances, the best course of action may be to avoid further engagement with these sources.

Believe me, you could achieve similar outcomes through a strong belief and the right actions guided by mathematical, logical, analytical, or scientific thought processes, all without the need to consult these individuals.

The existence of God is a subject of debate, and if indeed God exists, it is likely that there would be no favouritism or the possibility of bribing Him through offerings, money, fruits, rituals, or direct visits.

In my perspective, it is possible that humans have created the concept of God or that astrology, in some cases, could be viewed as a dubious endeavour.

Politicians use the word Religion and Encash their Needs: Politicians often exploit the concept of religion for their own agendas. However, it's essential to remain secular and recognize that religion, or dharma, has been created by humans throughout history as a means to promote societal well-being and a peaceful and secure way of life. It's crucial to understand that no religion advocates harm to others; such harmful interpretations are human creations.

Every religion is rooted in a set of values, and it's important to respect these values. Avoid fixating on any particular dharma or religion, as this can negatively impact your mindset. Keep your mind free of prejudice.

Consider this example: when your hand is hurt, your mind tends to focus on the pain in your hand rather than the healthy functioning of other organs like your heart, brain, liver, kidneys, eyes, etc. Similarly, if you harbour negative thoughts or hatred towards a religion or group of people, your mind will dwell in negativity, hampering your success and peace of mind. This can impede your ability to concentrate on your goals.

It's advisable to maintain positive thoughts about all religions for your own benefit, not with the aim of changing the world. As I've repeatedly mentioned, the world reflects your own thoughts, and adopting this attitude can help you interact positively with individuals from any religious background.

Digital / Internet Mafia/ Online Coaching Gurus:

In today's digital age, it's important to be aware of how online platforms like Google track your interests and weaknesses. There are self-proclaimed gurus and supposed extraordinary thinkers who subscribe to YouTube advertisements and operate multiple websites, all in an attempt to capitalize on your vulnerabilities by presenting enticing visions of a colourful future.

You might have come across these types of advertisements:

- Struggling to make money despite putting in hard work? Click below for a quick solution. They often offer a brief speech and later ask you to subscribe or attend a session for a nominal fee.

- Dreaming of becoming a millionaire starting with just Rs 25,000 (approximately 300+ USD) per month? Click below to watch a video.

- Convinced that owning a house is a bad idea and want to become a millionaire in a few months? Join a webinar for just Rs 99 (about 1.5 USD).

- You may have seen videos on YouTube featuring someone driving a Ferrari, claiming they're living a worry-free life on a luxurious UK vacation with their family. They invite you to click below and join a webinar for just Rs 199 (around 2.5 USD).

These amounts may seem insignificant, and scammers are well aware of this. They target a mass audience, assuming that a percentage will subscribe. For example, if 500,000 people watch the video and 100,000 subscribe for Rs 99, the earnings can reach nearly 1 crore INR (approximately 140K USD). It's a substantial sum in India.
However, it's important to be cautious. Many of these webinars and sessions are filled with empty promises and impractical advice that won't truly change your life. I would recommend researching the background, career path, and life history of the respective speaker before subscribing. Not everyone who promotes such webinars has achieved genuine success.

Most of these individuals claim to have left their salaried jobs, but what's interesting is that they have ventured into internet coaching, purportedly to make people like you successful. However, it's important to exercise caution as the authenticity of their claims can often be questionable. In fact, if you delve into their histories, you may find that they either left their jobs voluntarily or were let go at a relatively early stage.

Success is not achieved through shortcuts; there are no free rides in this world. The path to success requires hard work, but it's also about working smart. Making it possible demands constant effort, meticulous planning, and careful forecasting. **Remember, success is not an overnight phenomenon; it's a journey that unfolds gradually.**

To gain valuable insights into achieving success, consider watching interviews with accomplished individuals such as Sachin Tendulkar, Amitabh Bachchan, Ratan Tata,

Steve Jobs, Warren Buffet, and studying the life stories of visionary leaders who built companies like Honda, KFC, Wipro, and more.

Don't miss to watch Hyundai Chung Ju-Yung's life story and the way he built a large enterprise are indeed remarkable.

By doing so, you can gather a wealth of knowledge that will aid you in planning for a successful future.

Friends & Relatives:

The situations involving astrologers or priests can't be generalized, and I prefer not to generalize them. I would estimate the probability at around 50%.

It's essential to understand that no one can solve your problems or fulfil your desires on your behalf. You are the key to solving your problems because, in many cases, you may be the cause of them. To achieve what you want, you must plan and take the right actions.

When you discuss your problems or weaknesses with someone, such as friends or relatives, you can expect various responses as listed below,

- Some may bring up past actions or events that they believe contributed to your current situation.

- Certain individuals may attempt to exploit your weaknesses for their benefit.

"Man lighting his Cigar from the burning house"

- Others might offer detailed descriptions of your problem, emphasizing the challenges you're facing.
- Many individuals will simply listen without providing significant input.
- **Unfortunately, some may gossip or spread news of your issues to others.**
- Sympathy may be expressed by some.
- **A few might compare their own experiences to yours, attempting to prove their own luck.**
- The most helpful responses usually come from a select few who offer practical recommendations for solutions.

In most cases, these interactions result in,
- No concrete actions taken.
- A lack of actionable solutions.
- Increased confusion.
- Unfavorable comparisons and feelings of unfairness.
- Heightened problem complexity.
- Worsening financial issues if money-related.
- Strained relationships, especially when others get involved.

These scenarios may vary in your own life, but they highlight the common outcomes of sharing personal challenges.

Movies:

Some movies are funded by political parties, religious organizations, industries, and other entities with specific agendas. These films are often created to serve as propaganda tools, evoke emotional responses, weakness, instill feelings of insecurity in the masses to further their respective interests. It's essential to be cautious of such movies, particularly those that focus on religion or target specific communities, as they may not always present an unbiased perspective.

Practice the below suggested list of items to be stronger and not to be weak due to the problems & challenges you are facing.

Keep Privacy no need to showoff:
Living a purposeful life means prioritizing your responsibilities and being cautious about sharing your personal or private details. It's crucial to remember that discussing certain matters, no matter how close you are to someone, can lead to unnecessary troubles.

Family Personal matters or relationship challenges
While there may be occasions when sharing becomes necessary, it's essential to carefully consider discussing deeply personal matters. If you find yourself in need of guidance or assistance, seeking the help of authorized counselors is often a better course of action.

You definition of purpose of life
Each person has their unique life experiences and perspectives, which can either enrich or distort your sense of life purpose.

Your goals and future vision
People have varying life goals, and your aspirations may appear ambitious to others, possibly making you seem greedy. However, this perception often results from discussing your goals and future vision with individuals who may not understand your perspective. It's advisable to share such thoughts with someone who has experience in the same area or can provide guidance.

About your wealth and cash flows
When you openly discuss your wealth and financial situation, there's a risk that this information may spread through word-of-mouth, potentially resulting in unwanted consequences.

It can also lead to an increase in the number of insincere individuals around you. However, genuine people will remain by your side regardless of your wealth and financial status.

Furthermore, the person you confide in might take advantage of your financial situation by requesting favors or assistance.

About your investments

If you discuss your investments with others, you may receive advice that encourages you to divert your investments elsewhere. While this advice might offer short-term benefits, it could lead to various ways in which the person may exploit you, ultimately resulting in significant long-term losses.

Miracles in your Life – if you had any

If you have experienced a miracle in your life, it's often best to keep it to yourself. Sharing such experiences may lead others to perceive you as foolish, or they might attempt to replicate your actions, becoming envious if they don't achieve the same results.

Your Movements & Status in Social Networks

Always keep in mind that you are here to fulfill your responsibilities and live a purposeful life. There's no need to share every detail of your personal life on social networks such as WhatsApp status, Facebook, Instagram, YouTube, etc. Such information can be easily misused, often in ways that are hard to detect.

I would like to share 2 stories were Discussing about our and other personal or financial status would lead to dangerous effect.

Story #1:
A tragic incident occurred when a girl openly discussed her father's financial status in public. Unfortunately, someone overheard this conversation and intruded into her home. In the heat of the moment, her father confronted the intruder and tragically lost his life.

Story #2:
Another heart-wrenching incident involved a girl who lost her life due to disclosing personal matters to her classmates. This girl resided with her elderly parents in a rented house owned by a wealthy individual. She frequently discussed the financial status of the house owner with her classmates. One of her classmates, who came from a financially disadvantaged background, aspired to join UPSC exam coaching but lacked the necessary funds. In a desperate attempt to secure money, he hatched a plan with a friend to kidnap the owner's son. However, their criminal activities were eventually discovered, leading to devastating consequences. The girl not only lost her life, but her actions also plunged her entire family into turmoil.

Then how to come out from the state of Weak mind or Problems:
Re-iterating the sayings from Chapter#5:
"The universe plays no favourites; it's the individual who decides to be lucky or unlucky based on their Thought Process."
~Raghavendra Prasad MG

I can guarantee you that if you have a good purpose in your mind, you can achieve it through unwavering belief.

Re-iterating the sayings from Chapter#5:
"Individuals must take ownership of the problems they face."
~Raghavendra Prasad MG

"You are both the reason and the solution to your problems and disappointments."

~Raghavendra Prasad MG

When you feel you are weak in mind, list out the below and act up on accordingly.

Why? | Reason:
> Understanding the reasons behind your challenges and difficulties.

Other factors might be on Health | Family | Financial stability | Relationships:
> Recognizing that these factors can contribute to your situation.

Impact:
> Assessing the consequences of your current circumstances.

Talk to yourself on the above 3 items and Seek for Possible Solutions:
> Engaging in self-reflection and seeking solutions for your challenges.
> If solutions aren't apparent, consider seeking help from experts or professionals, even if it involves a cost.

Practice Road Map:
> Create a structured plan for improvement.
> Visualize and vividly picture your goals, then firmly store them in your mind.

Keep Iterative Improvement Plan:
> Embrace a continuous improvement mindset.
> Have a Milestone to Measure Success (say weekly or fortnightly):

Set measurable goals to track your progress.
Ensure You Are Meeting the Milestones:
Actively work towards achieving your milestones.

Execution should be in Agile – Keep the End Result in Mind:
Be adaptable in your approach while keeping your ultimate goal in mind.

Sometimes You Might Have to Revisit the Plan – That's Fine:
Be open & Agile to adjusting your plan as needed.

> **"Prioritize self-care, keep yourself fit, healthy, be confident, nurture responsible relationships, and work towards financial stability."**

This chapter summary can be depicted as below,

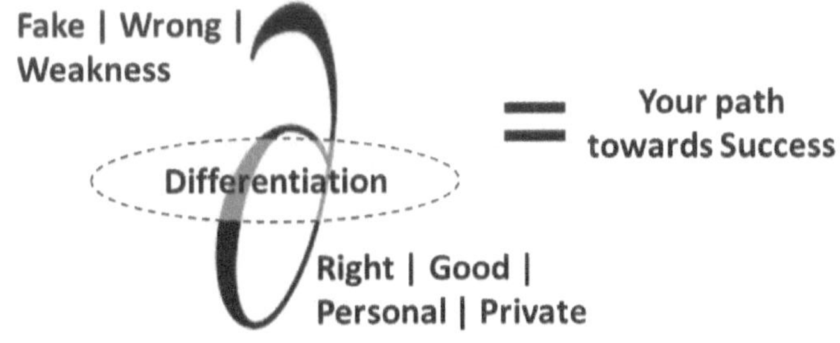

Couple of sayings from the experienced people, proverbs or philosophical teachings in the context of this chapter,

"Privacy is power. What people don't know; they can't ruin."

"In this era of digital everything, privacy is a precious commodity."

"Strength and growth come only through continuous effort and struggle."

~Napoleon Hill

"Strength does not come from physical capacity. It comes from an indomitable will."

~Mahatma Gandhi

"Weakness of attitude becomes weakness of character."

~Albert Einstein

"When everything seems to be going against you, remember that the airplane takes off against the wind, not with it."

~Henry Ford

"Admitting your weaknesses is the first step to growing stronger."

"Out of difficulties grow miracles."

~Jean de La Bruyère

"Recognizing your weaknesses is a strength."

"The greatest weakness of all is the great fear of appearing weak."

~Jacques-Bénigne Bossuet

"You are not your weaknesses; they are just areas waiting for growth."

"Weakness may be your weakness, but admitting it's your weakness is your strength."

~Luke Richardson

"The only thing we have to fear is fear itself."

~Franklin D. Roosevelt

"Embrace your weaknesses, for they are the foundations of your strengths."

"Appear Strong When you are Weak | Appear Weak when you are Strong".

~Chinese proverb

Personal Notes & Learnings

CHAPTER#13:
Stay away from Negative & Fake People!

"When the wrong or fake people leave your life, the right things start to happen."

~Buddha

"Wrong People teach right lessons."

~Buddha

This chapter will not only help you identify negative and fake people but also provide insights on how to deal with them, assuming that you are smart enough to learn from the experiences, observations & logical Analysis on the patterns and trends they use to follow.

This chapter may not be universally applicable to everyone. Only a fortunate few are blessed with an excellent environment (such as a good living space, supportive family, friends, partners, and children). In general, each of us has likely encountered situations where we failed to identify individuals attempting to take advantage of us. The intention of this chapter is not to mislead or create a negative mindset in anyone. Instead, it aims to empower you and encourage you to be extra cautious when dealing with people around you. Importantly, it should not negatively impact your relationships with those who genuinely care about you.

Furthermore, you may have unwittingly developed negative effects based on environmental factors and surroundings. This chapter can help you identify and overcome these effects as well.

People often manipulate others using their appearance, intelligence, power, confidence, capabilities, beliefs, and emotions through subjective discussions and false perceptions. It's crucial to be cautious of such individuals, especially those engaged in gaslighting, which is often done by two types of people:

Negative People: These individuals might belittle your intelligence, appearance, or capabilities, often within your own home environment.

Fake People: They employ tactics such as making you feel guilty, using excessive affection (honey trapping), and offering excessive praise (flattery), making you feel secure virtually to manipulate you and make you do as per their plan.

The likelihood of encountering a form of gaslighting known as 'flattering' is higher when forming close friendships with people who are financially stronger than you. Similar dynamics can also be observed in organizations as well. **Remember that when you are needed, you are most important. If not, your commitments, challenges, and so on may go unnoticed, and no one may care.**

Sweet Slow Poisonous People: These individuals' primary intention is to keep you happy, and nothing else. By ensuring your happiness and comfort, they aim to have you accompany them consistently, assisting in their day-to-day needs. Indirectly, they benefit from your knowledge and experience, applying it to their personal and professional growth. They may openly acknowledge that your presence has contributed to their success.

You may feel exceptionally comfortable and secure around these individuals. However, if you look back after some years, you may find that they have progressed while your life remains relatively unchanged. In reality, you have indirectly contributed to their growth. Beware of such people.

A typical indicator to identify these individuals is their reaction when you face trouble, losses, or problems. They may easily console you and make you so comfortable that you forget to reflect on your situation and take action to resolve your issues. You might start believing in an illusion that being with this person can solve all your problems. It's essential to recognize that this is your own misconception.

This effect can occur not only within personal relationships but also in the workplace. For instance, you may receive appreciations, awards, and recognition for your hard or smart work, yet find that you're not experiencing growth financially or in terms of your position. Meanwhile, your responsibilities increase steadily, while you observe your boss progressing.

I want to share a story about the largest organization in the same context. There were two colleagues, let's assume their names are X and Y, working together in the same company. X was very intelligent and a hard worker, while Y was intelligent and could be called smart or cunning, depending on individual perception.

Y said to X, "Let's start our own firm, and you can join me as a partner. We'll share the ownerships & profits equally." They joined together, and the small firm grew into a big enterprise. X worked day and night, implementing numerous strategies and products, while Y focused on marketing, sales, identifying market needs, and handling the legal aspects of the organization.

X dedicated over 20+ years of his life to these endeavours, forgetting about his family in the process, as he believed he owned the company. However, one day, Y fired X, as legally, X had no rights to the company. When X returned home, he found that his wife had left, and he didn't know where his children were. This tragic turn of events led X to take his own life.

This story clearly illustrates how X was made to work tirelessly for Y, neglecting his family and believing he had ownership of the company when, in reality, he did not. **Therefore, it serves as a warning to be cautious of bosses and friends who may exploit your dedication. The key lesson is to make the right decisions and work toward your own success, ideally in a mutually beneficial partnership.**

These individuals can be likened to alcohol, smoking, or mild drugs. Initially, their words and behaviour may provide a sense of thrill or security, much like the temporary effects of these substances. However, over the long term, their influence can prove detrimental, hindering your personal growth and leaving you without any lasting profitability or security.

Keep this in mind,

> **"If you are useful then enemy will become a friend and vice versa is also true, that is if you are no use, your close friend will also avoid you and it's not surprising if profitable he will become enemy."**
>
> **~Sri Krishna**

> "You have everyone to share in the profits and benefits, but no one to bear or share the losses."
> ~ Raghavendra Prasad MG

Identifying such manipulative individuals is essential. For instance, if you notice that a friend or anyone who constantly flatters you hasn't positively impacted your life within a reasonable timeframe (say, 3 - 6 months), and they are progressing while you're not, it's a sign that you might be falling into their trap. It's crucial to strategically distance yourself from such individuals.

Conversely, I have witnessed very few great people or good leaders who help their subordinates grow to their level, even though they may lose their jobs due to redundancy. At that moment, it might seem like a foolish decision. However, when viewed from a broader perspective and in the long run, these acts of goodwill have yielded amazing results in their personal lives.

Sometimes, you might engage in gaslighting behaviours yourself, either consciously or unconsciously, driven by factors such as fear of loss, insecurity, instability, lack of confidence, and other concerns. This book can help you recognize and address both situations, whether you're being manipulated or manipulating others.

Gaslighting can take various forms, including:
Isolation: Physically and mentally separating you from your environment and support system.

Confusion: Providing conflicting information that deviates from reality.

Fabrication: Creating false data or evidence to support their claims.

Repetition: Repeatedly presenting false information until you accept it as truth.

Guilt-Tripping: Some individuals employ guilt-tripping tactics to pressure you into doing what they want in the interest of their benefits. This often occurs within the context of family or even close friendships. For instance, a mother might tell her son, 'After you get married, no one will be here to take care of me,' or a friend/ relative consistently claims to be facing a financial crunch and makes you cover the restaurant bill or do a financial favour every time.

These tactics are subjective and rooted in the perceptions of those who employ them, and they are not necessarily true. Several examples demonstrate that individuals who faced such negative influences.

Mind Manipulation: It's an art of influencing someone's thoughts and actions through strategic conversation. For instance, consider this simple exercise: if I mention the word "food" or talk about eating, hotels, restaurants, etc and then ask you to fill in the blank for the word SO_P, you'll likely think of "SOUP."

Similarly, if I discuss topics like "Brushing" or "Bath" and then ask you to fill in the blank for the word SO_P, you'll probably still think of "SOAP." This is an example of how people can manipulate your mind, steering your responses in a particular direction that serves their interests.

Mind manipulation techniques can be used by individuals to control or influence others' behaviour, often to achieve their own objectives. Being aware of these tactics can help you guard against unwanted influence and make more informed decisions.

To protect yourself, it's essential to become less accessible to those who pull you down or treat you disrespectfully.

Don't let anyone disrupt your peace of mind. If you allow your mind to be disturbed, it can lead to poor decision-making and misfortune.

While it's impossible to avoid such people entirely, you can learn how to handle them effectively. Remember that no one else should define who you are; you must know yourself, your capabilities, desires, and goals.

To identify fake people, look for characteristics like inconsistency, exaggeration, insincerity, lies, manipulation, and wrong intentions.

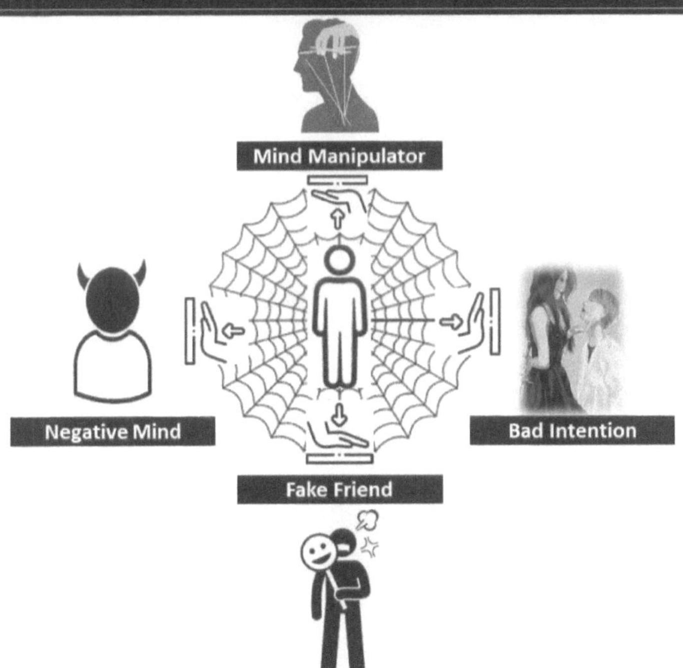

The evolutionary process demonstrates the Earth's continuous adaptation and progression. From single-cell organisms to complex creatures, and eventually to humans, life has evolved over time. This evolutionary journey serves as a reminder that the Earth is constantly changing and advancing.

Let's list out couple of animals and birds along with their behavior/ nature / skill set,

- **Dog**: Honesty
- **Cat**: Intelligent, always active
- **Lion**: Brave, teamwork, strategy, leadership
- **Tiger**: Independent, Solitary Hunter
- **Cheetah**: Speed
- **Snake**: Poison
- **Sparrow & Myna** – Loyal to partner
- **Fox**: Cunning & Intelligence
- **Eagle**: Exceptional Eyesight
- **Buffalo**: Unity, Empathy, Inclusion
- **Ants**: Hard work, Planning, Organization, Commitment
- **Elephant**: Team bonding, co-operation
- **Penguins**: Sharing responsibility, Job rotation
- Some female birds practice multiple partners and show little care for their offspring; instead, male birds often take on the caregiving role.
- Some bird species lay their eggs in other birds' nests and leave them to be raised by those birds.
- Some animals and birds may kill their own offspring.
- In many animal and bird species, males typically do not contribute significantly to raising their offspring.
- **Amphibians** and reptiles often do not even remember where they've laid their eggs and show no interest in caring for their offspring.

Overall, we can derive the following lessons from observing various animals:
- Teamwork
- Leadership
- Communication Skills
- Consistency
- Independent

- Responsibility
- Sharing
- Loyalty to Partners
- Ownership
- Dedication
- Creating a Support System
- Responsibility + Accountability
- Initiative + Decision-Making
- Empathy + Sensitivity
- Follow Standard Processes
- Standard Operating Procedures (SOP)
- Alignment with Environmental Conditions
- Poisonous | Aggressive – For survival and self defense

These lessons, drawn from the behavior and characteristics of animals, can provide valuable insights into various aspects of human life and behavior.

When a person approaches you, it's not just an individual; it's as if an entire kingdom of animals & birds is coming your way.

Human beings, the latest guests on Earth, have evolved from simpler life forms over time. Before humans, many animals and birds ruled and continue to exist on this planet. Humans often assert themselves as the protectors of the Earth with the slogan 'Save The Mother Earth.'

However, one may question whether humans truly have the authority to save the Earth, as Earth itself has its mechanisms for survival.

It's true that humans share common ancestry with other animals, and certain instinctual behaviors and responses are deeply rooted in our evolutionary history. When interacting with various animals, we often have an instinctual understanding of their potential actions based on their body language, behavior, and our collective knowledge of these species.
For example:
- When a dog is coming towards you: Many people can anticipate that a friendly dog might approach with a wagging tail, while an aggressive dog may display signs of hostility, such as raised hackles or growling.
- When a lion or tiger is coming towards you: In the wild, we recognize that these large predators may be approaching with predatory intent, and our instincts often tell us to be cautious and try to avoid confrontation.
- When a cow is coming towards you: Cows are generally considered docile and peaceful animals, so when a cow approaches, we may assume it is seeking food or simply curious.

These instinctual reactions to animals' behaviors are a result of our shared evolutionary history and the collective knowledge that has been passed down through generations. It's a testament to our ability to understand and respond to cues from the animal kingdom based on observation and instinct.

The complexity of the human thoughts, intentions, and emotions can be far more intricate and unpredictable compared to interactions with animals. Indeed, understanding human behaviour can be challenging, and it's important to approach interactions with an open mind and a degree of caution.

Here are some recommendations for dealing with the people:

First remember, "What you see is perception; what you hear is opinion. Therefore, see the world as it is."

Emotional Independence: It's essential not to let your own emotions be completely controlled by others. Maintaining emotional independence can help you make rational decisions and avoid being manipulated.

Confidentiality: While it's important to build trust in relationships, it's also crucial to be cautious about sharing sensitive information. Not everyone may have your best interests at heart, so exercise discretion in revealing personal details and secrets.

Non-Judgment and Acceptance: People change over a period of time based on the kind of experience and consequences they face hence Judgement on someone does not make sense,

Remember,
"Judge not, that you be not judged." (Extract from Bible).

"Doubt Everything, Do Not Judge."

"Every Sinner has a Future & Every Saint has a Past"
it's often better not to rush to judgment when trying to understand a person's motivations and actions. Accepting people as they are, while maintaining healthy boundaries, can lead to more harmonious interactions.

Financial Transactions: Exercise prudence in financial matters, as some individuals may exploit emotions, favorism, or love to gain advantages in financial transactions. Ensure you understand the terms and implications of any financial arrangement thoroughly.

Never Guage anyone by their appearances: A notable example can be seen in Cuckoo Bird – it's praised for its appearance and Voice talent. However, Cuckoo is entirely unethical; it lays its eggs in another bird's nest and its chicks will often throw the eggs or chicks out of the nest of other birds. Conversely, a crow is generally disliked due to its appearance, but it exhibits a good nature of sharing food with others.

> **"Evaluate friend Not by appearances and also not on just by how he talks ... gauge by his values, actions, integrity factors & his Intentions."**
> **~Raghavendra Prasad MG**

In summary, while humans may be the most complex creatures on Earth, navigating human interactions requires a balance of trust, caution, and empathy. It's important to approach each individual with an open mind while also safeguarding your own well-being and interests.

"You will attract people based on their needs than people who are willing to give you something, so it's important to keep mutual benefits in mind."

– experiment this statement, Monitor the below for next one week,

People come to you or call you**	1. For your benefit (X) 2. For their benefit (Y) 3. Informal (Z) (e.g., Friends, Relatives) 4. Formal/Neutral (e.g., Official)
People you go to or call**	5. For your benefit (A) 6. For their benefit (B) 7. Informal(C) (e.g., Friends, Relatives) 8. Formal/ Neutral (e.g., Official)
Note: Family calls Not considered**	

"For healthy and symbiotic relationships, ensure a balanced exchange of mutual benefits, ideally reaching equilibrium."

Below is the Mathematical Formula for the same,

$$(X - Y - Z) + (A - B - C) = \sim 0$$

"Giving without receiving – Leads to Frustration"
"Receiving without Giving – Leads to raise in Expectation"

Understand and Establish a Robust Support System:
Begin by comprehending the roles of the people around you in the following diagram and determining how to interact with and appreciate them.

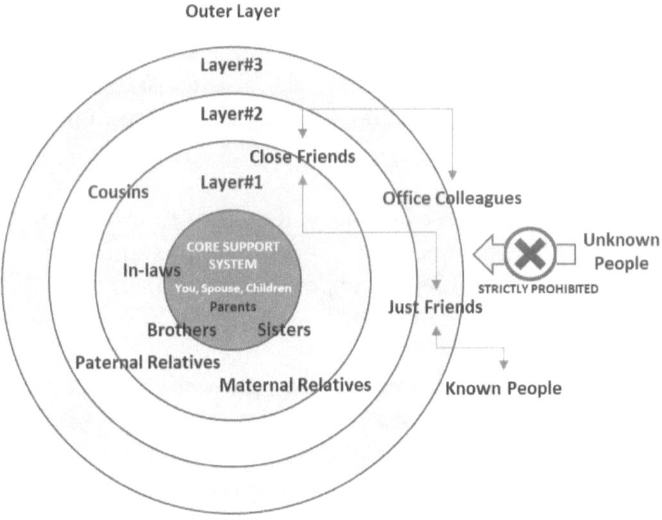

Always keep in mind that your responsibilities should take precedence above all else.

Imagine that if anything were to happen to you, it would significantly affect your Core Support System. Therefore, it's crucial to build a strong Core Support System and prioritize it, while also being discerning about who you allow into it.

How to Address Negativity and Inauthenticity in Your Support System:

Conversely, you yourself are a culmination of the entire animal and bird kingdom. It's not you – its 100's of versions of you within you. Your decisions are influenced by the consequences you've faced and the experiences, lessons you've learned in the past.

Buddha was well known to emanate a profoundly positive vibration wherever he went, and it was said that nothing negative would occur in his presence.
By observing Buddha and listening to his teachings, Angulimala, who was once a ruthless terrorist, underwent a profound transformation into a person committed to nonviolence.

Another illustrative example is the story of Amrapali, a professional prostitute who transformed into a nun due to the positive vibrations she experienced from a monk who was a follower of Buddha.

You can very much change the surroundings especially your core support system – through your positive vibrations.

Nature Synchronization: You might have noticed fireflies flashing their lights simultaneously with those of their neighbours. Similarly, if your vibrations are strong, the people around you tend to resonate with your energy. Conversely, if your vibrations are weak, you may find yourself aligning with the vibrations of others.

Cultivating a positive attitude, embracing good values, and nurturing genuine intentions can help create a positive atmosphere within your support system. This positivity can significantly influence your immediate surroundings. It's essential to apply this primarily within your support system rather than trying to change the world. The intention of this book is not geared toward changing the world either. – remember you are NOT a Buddha, Basavanna, Jesus or a Prophet to change the world.

The list of examples showcases great personalities who emerged successfully despite facing negative influences:

Superstar **Rajinikanth** was once told that he could never become a film star while working as a bus conductor. He defied the naysayers and achieved greatness.

Amitabh Bachchan faced criticism for his tall stature but overcame it through unwavering determination and hard work.

The founder of **Honda**, after numerous failures, likely heard discouraging words, yet he believed in himself and succeeded.

The entrepreneur who launched **KFC** in his old age may have encountered scepticism, but his determination led to global success.

These examples highlight the importance of not letting others' perceptions define your potential.

Even a child who struggled academically in school can become a renowned scientist, thanks to the unwavering support of a loving mother at home.

In a similar way, that same innocent child, when nurtured positively, can grow into a patriot who sacrifices for their country, benefiting society.

Conversely, in contrast to the above examples, a child born with innocence can be negatively influenced, potentially leading down a destructive path, such as terrorism, which ultimately harms society.

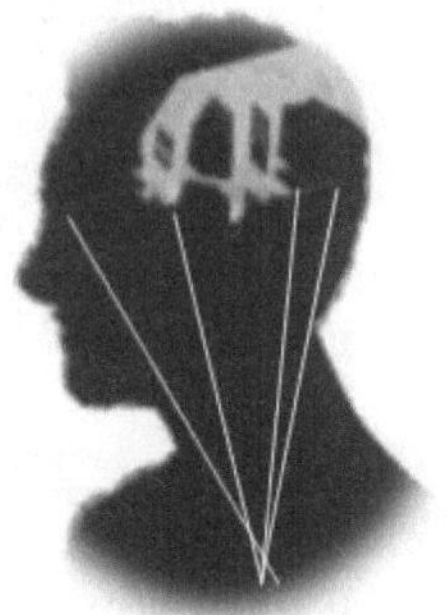 

To overcome negative/fake and gaslighting effects, follow these 15 rules strictly, drawing from the teachings of Sri Krishna in the Bhagavad Gita & Chanakya in Artha Shastra:

1. Believe in your capabilities.
2. Control your desires and emotions.
3. Avoid making decisions in anger or haste.

4. Understand that nothing comes for free; people rarely do favors without expecting something in return.
5. Cultivate a continuous learning mindset, Be Agile – Ready to accept the change.
6. Fear nothing.

7. Keep your weaknesses, future plans, and financial status private.
8. Find inner peace.
9. Fulfill your responsibilities promptly.
10. Always give your best effort, regardless of the outcome.

11. Trust that everything happens for the best.
12. Don't try to mimic anyone.
13. Avoid anything illegal or unethical.

14. Don't Judge or Gauge anyone

15. Finally, "Doubt everything", conclude based on the objective facts & realistic data points not or Perceptions, Opinions or through subjective discussions, emotions or guilt or sympathy.

"Time Discovers Truth"

~Seneca

Universe will itself will establish & reestablish righteousness (Dharma).

Sri Krishna Says,
"परित्राणाय साधुनाम विनाशय च दुष्कृतम् | धर्मसंस्था-पनाध्र्याय संभव-वामि युगे युगे"

("Pari-tranaya saadhunaam vinaa-shaya cha dushkrutam | Dharam samstha-panarthaya sambha-vami yuge yuge")

Meaning,
To protect the righteous (Dharma), to annihilate the wicked, and to reestablish the principles of dharma (righteousness, integrity, morality, uprightness), the power of the Divine will manifest, millennium after millennium, by the Laws of the Universe, appearing again and again.

Sri Krishna also says the below in Bhagavad-Gita,
धर्मो रक्षिति रक्षितः, अधर्मो भक्षितः

"Dharmo Rakshiti Rakshitaha | Adharmo Bhakshitaha"

Meaning,
"Dharma (righteousness) protects those who protect it. | Adharma (unrighteousness or wickedness) consumes or destroys those who follow a path of unethical & wrongdoings"

Couple of sayings from the experienced people, proverbs or philosophical teachings in the context of this chapter,

"Fake people have an image to maintain. Real people just don't care."

~ H. Jackson Brown Jr.

"Fake friends are like shadows. They follow you in the sun but leave you in the dark."

~Buddha

"Stay true to yourself. Fake people will eventually reveal their true colours. Keep shining, and let the fakes fade away."

"Don't be fooled by their mask. Fake people eventually show their true colours. Just wait until their mask needs cleaning."

Personal Notes & Learnings

CHAPTER#14:
Constant learning for stressless life with healthier relationships

"Give me six hours to chop down a tree and I will spend the first four sharpening the axe."
                                        ~Abraham Lincoln

"As long you live, keep learning how to live"
                                        ~Seneca

Once upon a time, there were two men (let's assume Wood Cutter #1, & Wood Cutter #2) who joined for wood-chopping work.
The payment depends on the number of trees being cut every day.
Their boss gave them axes and showed the area in the forest where they must work.

Since morning till evening both wood cutters worked and at the end of the day, they brought down the cutdown trees. Below is the statics which both wood cutters brought from the forest,

Day#	Wood Cutter #1 – Trees Delivered	Wood Cutter #2 – Trees Delivered
1	18 (8 Hours work)	15 (8 Hours)
2	16 (8 Hours work)	15 (8 Hours)
3	14 (8 Hours work)	15 (8 Hours)
4	13 (9 Hours work)	15 (8 Hours)

5	10 (9 Hours work)	15 (8 Hours)
6	9 (9 Hours work)	15 (8 Hours)
7	8 (10 Hours work)	15 (8 Hours)
8	7 (11 Hours work)	15 (8 Hours)
9	5 (11 Hours work)	15 (8 Hours)
10	3 (12 Hours work)	15 (8 Hours)

Wood Cutter #1 delivery went down drastically from 18 to 3 in 10 days of duration with the increase in the working hours.

Surprisingly Wood Cutter #2 maintained the consistency in delivering 15 Trees everyday with the same number of working hours.

Observations of both the wood cutters is shown below.

Wood Cutter #1 – Could not Deliver consistently	**Wood Cutter #2 - Delivered consistently**
Hard worker without planning & focus Stressed Feel pressured. No idea on Optimization, Efficiency, Productivity or smart work mechanism No time to his family and friends	Works 8 hours a day Smart worker Consistent, Efficient & Productive Invest time in planning. Optimize or maintain the execution time constant. No Stress Makes time for his family and friends.

How did it happen?

The answer is already there in the Abraham Lincoln saying.

The key point is Wood Cutter #2 use to spend 2 hours of day in sharpening his axe.

While Wood Cutter #1 is bothered about the outcome and believes on hard work. Never thought smartly, instead he would say I don't have time to sharp the axe.

Moral of the story:
"Taking time out to sharpen your skills constantly is worth many hours of hard toil."

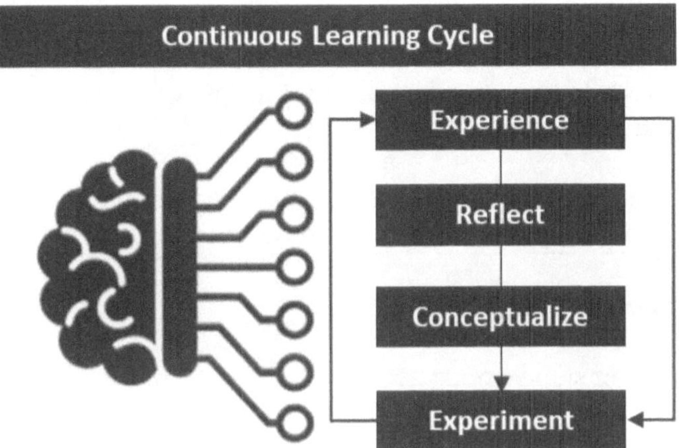

Sometimes, being a little quicker than those around you is sufficient; there's no need to be too fast.

I would like to tell you a small story which is little near to this chapter context, this story may not applicable in all the situation in life, but definitely you can use the moral of the story according to the specific situation you get for your benefits and need.

There were 4 Friends who went for a trekking in a thick forest. All walked for whole day, and they were kind of returning. while coming back then removed all their trekking shoes and walking by a lightweight slipper since the trekking shoes were quite heavy. suddenly a tiger appeared in front of them. everyone was panicked.

It might jump and eat them. out or 4 friends one friend started wearing shoes and preparing to run. one of them asked would you be able to run faster than a hungry tiger;

we are going to die. He calmly said - I am not sure about how speed the tigers comes near us but am sure and confident that I can run bit faster than you guys.

This is how just go with a flow based on the surroundings. you need not to have to over stressed by taking extra risk to reach the goal. **relax and enjoy the life journey based on the surroundings.**

Couple of sayings from the experienced people, proverbs or philosophical teachings in the context of this chapter,

"Learn > Adapt > Grow"

"Never stop learning because life never stops teaching."

"Live as if you were to die tomorrow. Learn as if you were to live forever."

~Mahatma Gandhi

"Learning is a treasure that will follow its owner everywhere."

"The day you stop learning is the day you stop living."
~Albert Einstein

"The capacity to learn is a gift; the ability to learn is a skill; the willingness to learn is a choice."
~Brian Herbert

"In learning, you will teach, and in teaching, you will learn."
~Phil Collins

"Learning never exhausts the mind."
~Leonardo da Vinci

"The beautiful thing about learning is that no one can take it away from you."

~B.B. King

"The only person who is educated is the one who has learned how to learn and change."

~Carl Rogers

"If you are not willing to learn, no one can help you. If you are determined to learn, no one can stop you."

~Zig Ziglar

"Education is not preparation for life; education is life itself."

~John Dewey

Personal Notes & Learnings

CHAPTER#15:
Simple living and high thinking

"Simple problems can be easily solved unlike complex problems – hence make your life simple & easy going"
~Raghavendra Prasad MG

"Materialistic or financial desires are far removed from simplicity; they seldom align."
~Raghavendra Prasad MG

"Simple living has no competition, ensuring satisfaction and keeping you away from the rat race of materialistic competition."
~Raghavendra Prasad MG

"Treating every individual as a human being, regardless of their social and financial status, reflects a simple living, high-thinking mindset."
~Raghavendra Prasad MG

Remember the following ground rules to embrace simple living and high thinking in your life to achieve your goals:

1. **Purpose Before Want or Need:** Prioritize your purpose over your desires and needs.
2. **Cultivate a Utility Mindset:** (For more details, refer to Chapter #16)
3. **Quality Lies in Simplicity:** Understand that the quality of life is found in simplicity.
4. **Happiness Is a State of Mind:** Your happiness doesn't depend on your status or wealth.
5. Complexity Leads to Confusion, Simplicity Doesn't.
6. **Materialism Hinders Goal Achievement:** Individuals with materialistic views may struggle to focus on their goals and achieve success.

7. **Dressing Style ✦ Greatness**: People with luxury dressing styles may not necessarily possess great minds. Consider figures like Mahatma Gandhi and Lal Bahadur Shastri, who dressed simply but had profound thoughts and ideologies.
8. **Prioritize Welfare Over Luxury**: Completely ignore the desire for a lavish lifestyle and focus on the welfare of society. An example can be seen in the life of Ratan Tata.
9. **Comparisons Diminish Happiness**: Simple living allows you to find happiness with limited resources, without the need to compare yourself to others.
10. Simple living leads to contentment in life.

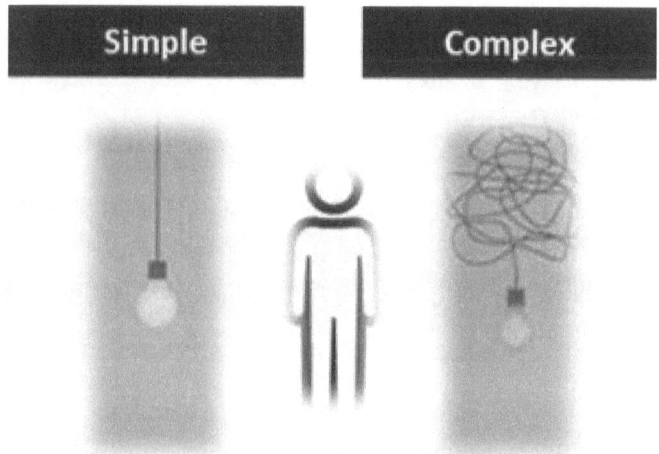

Benefits Of Simple living and high thinking:
1. You get more free time as you are not in a race or competition. – In turn you are free from stress, financial freedom, less commitment, less expectation leading to good relationships & continuous learning.
2. Simple living leads to conscious activities, spending time with yourself, self-reflection, inner peace & happiness, which will finally result in high thinking.
3. Simple living will facilitate you to think only about what is important to you without greed or damage to anyone (others or nature also)

The Story of a 99 coins club

Once there was a king, Due to lots of responsibilities he uses to feel stressed and pressured. Opposite to his Bedroom balcony he used to see a farmer who was very happy. He is happy with his farming and family, he lived with no stress, he used to work hard by enjoying his work and was contented with his life as well.

King always wondered and questioned himself how this farmer can be so happy, even after he doesn't have luxurious life. The king asked this his minister to find out the reason behind the farmer's happiness.

The minister observed that the farmer was happy because he didn't have anything to worry about. He used to work hard, to earn his bread and butter for the day, he never bothered about the future he is living in the present moment. because he uses to work hard, he gets good sleep. He was happy with his family and farming.

The minister kept a small bag of 99 gold coins in front of farmer's house. Next day when the farmer saw the bag, he felt blissful, started thinking God has listened to him, he is so fortunate, etc.

He and his wife started counting them. They did count multiple times, they concluded there were 99 coins.
The series of questions started arising in Farmer and his wife's mind.

What could've happened to that last gold coin? Surely, no one would leave 99 coins!' they were wondered. They started looking everywhere they could, but that final coin was no were found. Finally, they got exhausted and then they concluded God has intentionally made 1 coin short and God is instructing us to work harder to complete the coins collections to 100. And they decided to work hard to earn One gold coin.

From that day Farmer started to working very hard and hard and could not give enough attention to his family. He was completely focused on earning that one more coin. He stopped enjoying his work. The king observed this and asked his minister what happened to him, why is he no happier and more contended? The minister replied that he has joined our 99 coins club.

The 99 coins club is a name given to those people who have enough in their life to be happy with contentment, but they always feel restless to earn more and get more of it, having such an attitude - let me earn some more and then I will be happy and have a peaceful life, in reality it will never come.

Happiness is a state of mind, it cannot be achieved from materials. One can be happy with what they have today. When people run behind Rat race, competitions, comparisons? looking at others, he or She has it, I also should have it. I also prove that I am not less than him/ her. so, I should get it at any cost, no matter what I do, this is the attitude that today generation has.

When we say little more the output is straightaway, we will lose sleep, happiness, feelings with people around us, relationships, etc. as we are spending time or price on to our greedy mind -which can't see anything apart from saying "little more".

Couple of sayings from the experienced people, proverbs or philosophical teachings in the context of this chapter,

"The poor and the rich are equally food; the king and the servant are equally food."

~Basavanna

"Thinking broadly with a focus on great perspectives and appreciating the small things elevates your thought process."

"Avoid expensive fashion and show-offs; instead, use your wealth for the welfare of society and those in need."

"Simplicity will manifest in our behaviour, speech, manners, and nature."

"Small is Beautiful"

~E.F.Schumacher

"Make money and use it; do not let money use you."

~Basavanna

Personal Notes & Learnings

CHAPTER#16:
Principles of Success

"Balancing Responsibility & Then Relationships between Health and Earnings is an Art."

"Value responsible relationships not just relationships"

~Raghavendra Prasad MG

– as shown below,

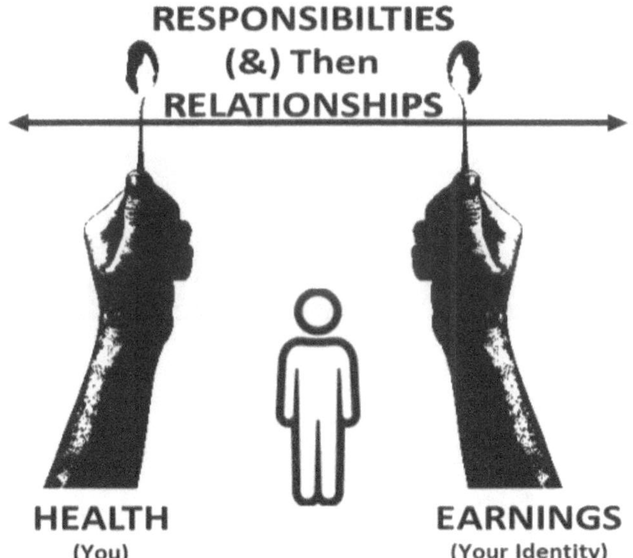

Follow 33%: 33%: 33% Rule in Life.

HEALTH	EARNINGS	RESPONSIBILTIES (&) Then RELATIONSHIPS
33%	33%	33%

Health:

Health plays a pivotal role and should be your top priority in life. It's the foundation upon which everything else is built. Your growth, ability to work, and earning potential all stem from good health. Your health played a role in attracting your spouse and ensuring a satisfying physical and mental connection. Moreover, your health is a vital factor in the well-being of your children. Therefore, never compromise on your health.

Earnings:

After securing your health, the next step is earning a living. Earnings provide you with an identity in society and enable you to fulfil various responsibilities, such as being a husband, father, son, and more. Without earnings, your identity in society becomes uncertain. Earnings are crucial and follow closely after your health.

Responsibilities & Then Relationships:

> "Start with your responsibilities; genuine relationships will naturally follow."
>
> ~Raghavendra Prasad MG

The title itself makes it clear: Responsibilities come before Relationships. It's essential to prioritize your responsibilities before entering into relationships. This isn't to say that relationships are unimportant, but rather that responsibilities take precedence. Responsibilities can encompass various aspects of life, including your role at work, within your family as a son, husband, or father, your responsibilities as a citizen to your country, and your role within society. It's crucial to understand your responsibilities and manage them wisely. These responsibilities can be categorized as mandatory, primary, secondary, or obligatory. The choice of how to manage them is yours to make, ensuring they align with your life's priorities.

"Prioritize responsibilities before relationships."

And when it comes to relationships, ask yourself if you are:

A good son A good brother A good husband A good father A good son-in-law A good friend	A good boss A good employee A good customer Good to country Good to nature

Realize that you cannot excel in all these aspects simultaneously. Setting high expectations can strain relationships. Instead, aim to expect nothing from others and maintain minimal expectations. Avoid trying to satisfy everyone through financial means, as it's an endless endeavour. Know your limits and think carefully before investing your time, money & energy in anything or anyone.

Strive for independence and minimize dependency on others. Lowering expectations to a minimum or even zero is often the best approach.

Dependent	Self-Dependent /Independent
Plant on Pot | Chord around a Tree	Standalone Huge Self Grown Tree

Dependent	Self-Dependent /Independent
Lion in Cage	Lion In Wild

Freeing Your Mind from Debts and Regrets:

In the universe, there's no concept of regret. Everything happens for a reason. Proceed with a positive outlook. To avoid falling into the traps of debts and regrets, consider the following:

- Strive for as much independence as possible.
- Adopt a mindset of expecting less. If you help someone, do so without expecting anything in return.
- Offer help to others within your capacity, but never stretch beyond your limits.
- Think carefully before seeking help from anyone. Remember, it's often a give-and-take scenario, and nothing is entirely free in this world. The Favor may be expected in return.
- Avoid financial transactions within relationships, as this can strain them.

It's important to debunk some common misconceptions:

- Pursuing money at the expense of health and relationships can be detrimental.
- Money alone can't buy good health when health issues arise.
- Attempting to repair relationships solely through financial means may not succeed.

"Money has, to a large extent, overshadowed other aspects of life. It's a bitter truth that many people attempt to buy health and relationships through money."

All three elements—health, wealth & responsibilities/ relationships are interconnected and must be balanced. Remember the age-old saying, 'Health is wealth.' Your health, both physical and mental, is of utmost importance. Your mental well-being depends on how you manage your responsibilities, relationships, and earnings. These three segments are interconnected and influence each other. When one is affected, it has a ripple effect on the other two, as illustrated in the diagram below,

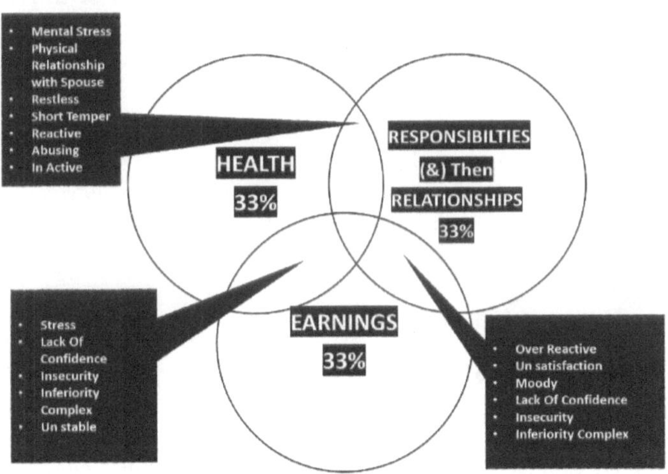

It's possible to find a compromise between money and relationships to some extent, with a small variation of 10-15% here and there. For instance, if your parents are unwell and need your time, it's essential to provide that care. Similarly, there may be critical work tasks that demand your attention and time.

However, it's crucial to question the duration of such compromises. Ideally, a period of 3-6 months is acceptable. If it extends beyond that, it's advisable to explore alternatives or reevaluate your priorities, ensuring you return to the 33%:33%:33% rule.

Keep in mind that time holds immense value, often more than money. Time, money & energy are similar when it comes to spending. So, be cautious about how you invest your time. While you can earn money at any point in life, you can never earn back lost time & energy being invested.

Embrace a Utility Mindset for Responsible Purchases:
When considering the purchase of any substantial item with liability, it's crucial to think carefully before making the investment. Let's take the example of buying a car, which is a significant liability. Before proceeding, ask yourself these key questions:

- Why am I buying this car?
- What is its intended purpose?
- What will be the total investment? (Cars come in a wide range of prices, from 4 lakhs to crores of rupees (INR))
- What are the monthly EMIs?
- What are the maintenance costs per month and per year?
- Can I comfortably afford it?

Understanding your purpose clearly ensures that your decision aligns with your needs. If you approach the purchase with a show-off mindset, you might experience initial excitement, but it could lead to significant challenges down the road.

> "Over spending beyond your limits with show-off mindset might lead to huge financial loss, being mis-utilized by someone, in the long run it might result in losing some one or even self as well"
>
> ~Raghavendra Prasad MG

Balancing Honesty with Caution:
"A person should not be too honest. Straight trees are cut first, and honest people are screwed first."

~Chanakya

While the saying 'Honesty is the best policy' holds true, it's essential to recognize that honesty is a two-way street. You are not obligated to be honest with individuals who do not reciprocate that honesty.

Honesty should be practiced judiciously, on a case-by-case basis. It's not a one-size-fits-all approach. You must be astute in handling different situations and people.

Importantly, consider the long-term consequences of your actions. If you are honest with someone who is not honest with you, you might:

- Be perceived as naive
- Be taken for granted
- Incur losses
- Have your emotions hurt
- Gain no benefits
- Damage relationships
- Being misused

It's crucial to balance honesty with wisdom, ensuring that your actions align with the situation at hand.

Distinguishing Business from Charity:
Dharma or charity and business are fundamentally distinct, and they should never be conflated or treated as the same. Treating them as such could result in significant financial losses and a loss of identity.

Allow me to share a beautiful story I heard from Swamy Nityananda, which opened my eyes:

As a young boy, Swamy Nityananda used to visit his grandmother's house during vacations. One day, his grandmother took him to a nearby market where a lemon seller was offering lemons for 5 Annas each. Through her negotiation skills, his grandmother managed to purchase 5 lemons for 20 Annas. Later, she realized that the lemon seller had been sitting in the scorching sun since morning, without having anything to eat. Without hesitation, she rushed home, prepared four idlis, sambar, and a cup of water, and offered them to the seller.

Young Nityananda wondered why his grandmother had haggled so much for a mere 4 Annas, but willingly offered food worth 20-30 Annas. When he asked her about it, she replied, **'Never mistake business and Dharma as the same. In business, we consider profit and loss, but in Dharma, we find joy in giving and derive satisfaction.'**

Therefore, it's crucial to maintain two mindsets—one for business and another for charity or Dharma—without mixing them.
These two paths lead in different directions:
- Business should lead to profit and mutual benefit.
- Charity or Dharma should lead to the joy of giving and satisfaction, without expecting financial gain.

Effective Associations:
In addition to your primary responsibilities and obligatory relationships, associations and socialization with others hold great significance. However, these interactions should align with one or more of the following criteria,
- Shared interests
- Mutual respect
- Mutual benefit
- Common field of work
- Knowledge exchange
- Point Of Views On life goals
- Most importantly, shared & common values

If your associations and socializing do not contribute to any of the items mentioned above, it's advisable to reconsider their value and consider discontinuing such associations.

It's not your responsibility to change or modify anyone else. Remember you are the Owner/ CEO of your life, you have a liberty to associate or disassociate with anyone, Accept the people as they are, Associate/ Disassociate, Hire, Fire and Promote accordingly to mutual benefits & respect, nothing harm here. It's good to both of you.

> **"Do Friendship by Values, Mutual interests & benefits Not by Social Status or Position." | "Associate with the People who improve you"**
> **~Raghavendra Prasad MG**

Good habits V/s Bad habits:

"We are what we repeatedly do. Excellence, then, is not an act, but a habit."

> **~Aristotle**

> **"Good habits lead to good health, prosperity, and fortune, while bad habits lead to poor health, loss, and misfortune."**
> **~Raghavendra Prasad MG**

In the same way,

"Good times may lead to bad times in the absence of discipline, whereas bad times can lead to good times with discipline."

Closely observe the below table on how Good Habits leads to good health, Prosperity and Fortune,

Good Habits	Bad Habits
Wake Up Early	No Timing
Regular Exercises	Optional
Manage time well, Fixed Time for every thing	No Time / anytime
Control over Eating	No Control/ sometimes
He is moving towards Financial Freedom unknowingly	He is moving away Financial Freedom unknowingly
Every situation is a learning	Every situation is challenging
Work towards Goals and Visions	Mostly No Goals and vision but have desires
Disciplined	Mostly Not Disciplined
People around you will also set to your Habits – leads to positive impact	People around you will also set to your Habits – leads to negative impact
You are seeding your life style in your next generation – leads to positive impact	You are seeding your life style in your next generation – leads to negative impact
Active	May be Lazy
Leads to Good Times	May Lead to Bad Times

Develop Beneficial Habits for Personal Growth:

To achieve success in life, cultivating good health habits and making sound daily decisions are crucial. Your future is shaped by your present choices and actions.

1. **Regular Exercise**: Engaging in regular exercise promotes longevity and physical fitness. Surveys indicate that approximately 88% of successful individuals exercise or perform aerobic activities at least three times a week. They understand that good health is paramount and shouldn't be compromised.

2. **Reading Books**: Reading books consistently helps you find solutions in your daily life. Read books on personal development, history, biographies of accomplished individuals, and books that aid decision-making. Over 75% of successful people read for at least 30 minutes daily or complete six to ten books each year. Reading before bedtime allows your subconscious mind to absorb and apply the knowledge you've gained.

3. **Learn to Say No: "You cannot be nice to everyone all the time"**, Don't hesitate to decline when you're uncomfortable with a situation. Learning to say no is vital for personal growth. Successful individuals are unafraid to reject uncomfortable circumstances.
"One Sincere Rejection is Far Better Than 1000 Fake Promises"

~Buddha

4. **Avoid Subjective Arguments**: Foster a habit of minimizing arguments, especially those rooted in subjectivity. While healthy debates can be productive, avoid engaging in arguments based solely on personal perspectives & opinions which are Subjective in nature.

5. **Maintain Relationships**: Remember to acknowledge and celebrate birthdays, send New Year wishes, and regularly check in with loved ones. Connecting with friends and family

through healthy and objective discussions enhances your well-being and decision-making abilities.

6. **Explore New Places**: Occasionally visit different locations, whether nearby villages, the outskirts of the city, old temples, or natural settings. Spending time in nature and observing the world around you can stimulate your thoughts and creativity.

7. **Interview Unfamiliar People**: Engage with unfamiliar individuals you encounter in your daily life, such as roadside vendors, cab drivers, or fellow commuters. Learn about their lifestyles, earnings, and how they balance their lives. This activity can offer insights into financial planning and life decisions.

8. **Watch Movies and Documentaries**: Set aside time to watch motivational movies and documentaries, at least twice a month. These films often provide valuable life lessons and guidance.

9. **Select Beneficial Friends**: Maintain friendships that offer mutual benefits and align with your interests. Choose friends who contribute to knowledge sharing and guidance, as these connections can broaden your perspectives.

10. **Avoid Short-Term Desires**: Refrain from developing habits centered on short-term gratification. Be mindful of activities that fall into this category.

11. **Develop Patience**: Cultivate patience as a daily habit. Remember that the Earth itself operates without haste, taking billions of years to evolve. Enjoy the journey of life and take your time.

12. **Long-Term Decision Making**: When situations are under control, choose options that consider long-term effects. Avoid decisions driven solely by short-term gains or desires. If a situation is beyond your control, maintain belief in

actions that benefit everyone's welfare and keep moving forward.

To achieve success, you must cultivate two essential qualities:
- Discipline
- Hard Work

> **"Discipline paves the way to freedom, while hard work leads to success."**
> **~Raghavendra Prasad MG**

Discipline can be likened to Newton's First Law of Motion, also known as the Law of Inertia, which states that **"An object at rest will stay at rest, and an object in motion will stay in motion at a constant velocity unless an unbalanced force is applied."** Similarly, when you develop a habit of discipline, you tend to adhere to it, as it aligns with the natural tendency to maintain one's current state.

"Your level of success is determined by your level of discipline and perseverance."

You might be wondering how discipline can lead to freedom. It's true. When you are disciplined, you become self-reliant. Your disciplined approach naturally encourages others to become self-sufficient as well. This applies to your subordinates at work, your children, other family members, or friends. This is how you liberate yourself from dependency on others' work, allowing you to focus on your own goals and take actions in line with your plans.

> **"Effective discipline can train your body to make decisions habitually or instinctively."**
> **~Raghavendra Prasad MG**

> **"Good discipline will Procrastinate / avoid negative or lazy things from you, which will result in positive results."**
> **~Raghavendra Prasad MG**

How Does Hard Work Matter?

Everything to be earned: Hard work is the key to obtaining everything in life, whether it's health, wealth, status, relationships, or other aspects.

Acquired Characteristics Over Genetics: While genetics play a role in determining traits like physical appearance, metabolism, intelligence, and sometimes wisdom, it's the acquired characteristics that often win the day. Successful individuals demonstrate that their hard work outweighs genetic factors. If you examine the lives of accomplished people, you'll find that they reached the pinnacle of success through relentless hard work.

Change is Inevitable: Remember, your current state is not your permanent state. Change is a fundamental law of nature. Through consistent hard work, you have the power to transform yourself and move toward success.

"Did you know that every particle in your body is replaced approximately every 7 years? This means that you are not the same person you were 7 years ago."

How much is Enough?
Would like you talk about one story here, about The Fisherman and the Businessman. Once upon a time there was a businessman who was sitting on the beach in a small Italian village. As he sat, taking a brief break from the stress of his daily schedule, he saw a fisherman rowing a small

boat back into the harbour. In the boat were a few large fish.

Impressed, the businessman asked the fisherman, "How long does it take you to catch so many fish?" To which he replied "Oh, not so long." The businessman was confused, "Why don't you fish for longer to catch even more?"

"More? This is enough to feed my entire family and even offer some to my neighbours," the fisherman said. "So, what do you do for the rest of your day?" Enquired the businessman. The fisherman replied, "Well, I've usually have caught my fish by late morning, at which point I go home, hug my wife, and play with my kids. In the afternoon, I read a newspaper & take a short nap. In the evening, I go to the village to have a drink with my friends, play guitar, sing, and dance into the night!"

Putting his entrepreneurial hat on, the businessman offered a suggestion. "I have a PhD in business! I can help you become much more successful. From now on, you should spend longer at sea and catch as many fish as possible. When you've saved enough money, buy a bigger boat to catch even more fish. From there, you'll soon be able to buy more boats, set up your own company, build a production plant to can the fish and control distribution, and move to the city to control your other branches."

To this, the fisherman asks, "And after that?"

The businessman laughs, "After that, you'll be able to live like a king, take your company public, float your shares and be rich!"

"And after that?" Asks the fisherman once more.

"After that, you can retire, move to a house by the sea, wake up early in the morning to go fishing, then return home to play with your kids, hug your wife, take a nap in the afternoon and join your friends in the village to drink, play guitar and dance into the night!"

Puzzled, the fisherman replies, "That's what I'm already doing?"

Moral:
The purpose of your life is very important and - How much is enough for me is very much important. In today's times We find so many people are in Rat race through competition saying want everything what is seen & I need better than what someone nearby has.

After responsibly taking care of life, do not miss to always celebrate abundance Joy & Happiness.

Would like to share another story on Contentment & Satisfaction
Once upon a time, there was a fisherman who led a calm and simple life. He had an assistant who often accompanied him while fishing. One day, the assistant informed the fisherman that he needed to visit a nearby city for personal reasons. Fisherman said I have a teacher who lives in the same city. The fisherman seized this opportunity and asked his assistant to seek an answer to a question: 'How can I find true satisfaction and contentment in life?'

The assistant traveled to the city and reached the luxurious home of the fisherman's teacher. He was amazed by the opulence surrounding him. The teacher warmly welcomed the assistant, treating him to royal hospitality.

The assistant conveyed his boss's question to the teacher, who chuckled and remarked, 'Your master is quite greedy.

He catches fish every day and always wishes he could catch more. This greediness prevents him from leading a contented life.'
The assistant was taken aback, thinking, 'This man has everything and yet calls my master greedy.' He then asked the teacher, 'Are you satisfied with your life?'
The teacher replied, 'Yes, I am.'

Curious, the assistant inquired further, 'Do you lead a contented life?'
The teacher confidently replied, 'Yes, I do.'

The assistant suddenly exclaimed, 'With all this luxury, anyone can live a satisfactory and contented life.'

The teacher responded, 'No, it's not about external possessions; it's a state of mind.'

Perplexed, the assistant invited the teacher to join him. The teacher agreed, and they walked together for about a mile. During their walk, the teacher enjoyed every moment, appreciating the surroundings and people they encountered. Suddenly, the assistant realized he had left his bag behind and insisted on returning to fetch it.

The teacher was surprised by this and said, 'You are still concerned about your belongings? I left everything behind to be in the present moment with you. I have let go of the past, but you are still attached to your past possessions. This is why your master is unsatisfied in his life. To find contentment, one must live in the present and let go of the past.'

Moral:
living in the present moment allows you to appreciate and find contentment with what you have.

Patience & Common Sense is most important then Strength:

It's an old story I read it in my childhood, but it has a life lesson. would like to share it with you.

Once upon a time, there was an old man with 4 Sons, all his sons were very lazy and never worked. one day old man died. There was no option left for all brothers apart from earn to live. they all decided to disperse and work hard for their survival and success, they decided one date after 5 years we all will come here and meet again and see who has achieved most. all agreed and left the place.

5 Years passed - they all came eagerly to the common place where they decided to meet 5 years ago.

All 4 brothers were so happy seeing each other and started sharing their journey of last 5 years. and they got in to challenging mode to prove themselves who is great among all. There was a Lion skeleton pieces laying here and there,

One of the brothers said, I know how to assemble the skeleton pieces, he did so. and another brother wanted to prove he is greater than him, he said I can create a Skin on top this lion skeleton and did so. another brother standing beside wanted to prove he is greater than others he said I can fill a flesh in to lion skin and did so, the last brother wanted to prove he is greater than all of them he said I can give a life to this lion... without even a second thought he gave a life to it... lion became live and killed all the brothers. that's how all brothers lost their life in proving that they are great...!

Moral:

Some time in our life as well, we are trying to prove something which is total useless, absolutely no sense on our decisions if you sit calmly and think. be Patient & apply

Common Sense rather than applying in a hurry with your strength, it results in damage than benefit.

Hasty decisions made you without applying common sense will not only put you in trouble but also create huge difficulties for your entire support system.

- as depicted in the below diagram.

Couple of sayings from the experienced people, proverbs or philosophical teachings in the context of this chapter,

"Discipline is choosing between what you want now and what you want most."

~Abraham Lincoln

"With self-discipline, most anything is possible."

~Theodore Roosevelt

"Discipline is the refining fire by which talent becomes ability."

~Roy L. Smith

"The price of excellence is discipline. The cost of mediocrity is disappointment."

~William Arthur Ward

"Discipline is the bridge between goals and accomplishment."

~ Jim Rohn

"Discipline is the foundation upon which all success is built. Lack of discipline inevitably leads to failure."

~Jim Rohn

Personal Notes & Learnings

Personal Notes & Learnings

CHAPTER#17:
Secret of long life

> "Choose a quality life over a comfortable life for a long and healthy life."
>
> ~Raghavendra Prasad MG

Quality life	Comfort Life
Wake up early, take a walk, and enjoy the sun, nature, and fresh air.	Wake up late, have a brewed coffee on the bed, sit on a super luxurious sofa, hold a mug of beer, and watch a movie in an expensive 4K home theater.
Happiness, Good health Guarantied if you are a simple living being.	Comfort may not provide happiness & Health
Self-dependent	Mostly Dependent
Clarity in Life	Complexity in Life

Understand Life's Laws & Principles:
It's essential to comprehend the laws and principles of nature and adjust your perspective towards life accordingly. Remember that stress is a natural part of life. Instead of reacting to every situation with the aim of making it go exactly as expected, **cultivate a "let it go" attitude and move forward.**

Challenges & difficulties are inevitable in life, whether you welcome them or not. How you choose to react, respond, and handle these challenges depends on your unique point of view. There are no rigid rules dictating how you should navigate these problems, as there's no universally right or wrong way to do so.

Always keep in mind that desirable aspects of life, such as good health, physical fitness, financial prosperity, and meaningful relationships, won't simply manifest on their own. You must actively work towards making them a reality, especially when faced with challenges and difficulties.

In your life journey, consider yourself a traveller passing through. Eventually, you will depart from this place and the people around you, leaving behind all material possessions. Embrace this perspective to appreciate the transient nature of existence and focus on what truly matters.

The Evolution of Point of View Towards Life:
A person's point of view towards life is shaped by various factors and often evolves over time. Here are some key influences on one's perspective,

Family Influence: Home is the first school, and parents play a crucial role in shaping a child's point of view towards life. Family values, behavior, and responses to situations significantly impact a child's early perspective.

Age and Life Stages: A person's interests, tastes, and point of view change as they progress through different life stages. For example, priorities may shift from food to relationships, career, health, and peace of mind at various ages.

Say for, Example#1: starting from birth till old age man run behind different things which depends on the age like starts from Food > Women > Comfort life / Earning / Identity > Health at middle age, handling Responsibilities/ full filling needs around relationships > Peace of mind, etc.

Changing Opinions on Relationships:

Relationships, especially the one with parents, often undergo transformations as a person grows older. A child's perception of their parents evolves, influenced by their age and life experiences.

Example#2: opinion on the same relationship will also change over a period of time, say a boy

- Around 5 – 6 years of age he feels his father knows everything and he is like a hero in his life,
- Eventually when he reaches 10+ years the same boy starts feeling Dad is quite harsh.
- By time he enters his teen age he starts feels that his father is getting changed
- When reaches secondary school he feels that he has lost his father of his childhood
- Then by Pre-University he feels he can't satisfy his father expectations, and also, he feels his friend's father is far better than his in terms of providing facilities, etc.
- When the boy gets into degree some small arguments crop up between the young boy and his father, eventually boy feels his father is stingy, rough, very difficult person to deal with, etc.
- Eventually he reaches around 25 – 27 he starts earning then he feels he knows much more than his father.
- The boy gets married at the age of 28 – 30 then there is a total miss match in the thought process between him and his father.
- He will have children > same cycle starts with his son about him as a father

- Finally, when he reached the age around 50+ he feels his father was so great and how much difficulties he has faced in his life to grow him up, etc. now again he feels proud of his father and he becomes Hero of his life again, but the time has gone, his father is no more at that time. this is how opinion/perception changes over a period on the same relationship.

Life Experiences: Significant life events and experiences can alter one's perspective on life. For instance, someone who once prioritized wealth or relationships may shift their focus to health after facing health-related challenges.
Say for example, A man running behind Women or Money/ Identity at some point of time say Health is more important than anything in a later stage!
Or a Person who has good health and happy family, would say money is very important, etc.

External Influences: In the modern world, external factors like the influence of peers, social media, and celebrities can have a profound impact on a person's point of view. People often get attracted to the lifestyles and identities of public figures Say for example, People look at a Film Star or a sports star and they get attracted to their identity and Comfort they have, they talk about their comforts more than their achievements, all about is most of us running behind comfort (Money) and then identity.

Food can be both Healthy & Unhealthy:
Food you eat with the below states will yield to good health,
- Having food when you are hungry
- Secured mindset.
- Blessed mindset
- Enjoying the food in a present moment
- Have food sitting in a comfortable place
- without talking to anyone

- without talking to phone
- without using phone
- Without watching TV
- Without reading newspaper or something
- Without thinking about work or commitments
- Without stress

I would say – While eating don't think or do any activity apart from enjoying the food. By doing so Your brain will understand that you are eating, and it will prepare the respective organs to receive the food properly and released happy hormones in turn it helps in good digestion and health.

If you are eating with stress, standing, doing other activities like talking, watching TV, phone, etc. your brain will concentrate on the other activities only which will not instruct the organs to receive the food resulting in obesity, unhealth, diabetes, etc.

Who is with you?
- Your Parents? – No
- Your Spouse? – No
- Your Children? - No
- Your Friends? – No
- Your Relatives? – No

Your Body and Mind:
Your physical and mental health are your constant companions throughout life. Taking care of them is essential for overall well-being.

As you age, your spouse often becomes a closer friend and companion. However, it's crucial to prioritize self-care and maintain a healthy body and mind.

Additionally, financial stability, represented by your saved money, can provide security and support in your later years.

In essence, nurturing a healthy relationship with yourself, maintaining good physical and mental health, and having a solid financial foundation can greatly enhance your overall quality of life and your ability to enjoy meaningful relationships with others.

Choose Best Out of available Options in life:
Sometimes, situations will arise where you need to prioritize specific options from a range of choices. It's not always possible to accommodate everything simultaneously. As illustrated in the diagram below, choose the best option among those you can afford and that aligns with your current status.

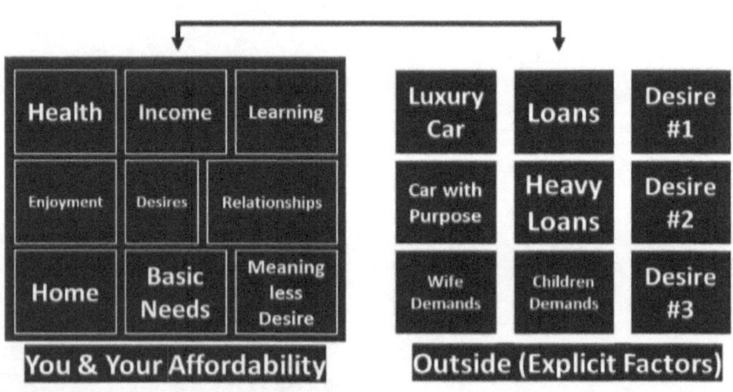

I wish everyone could become rich and famous so they realise it's not the answer

~Jim Carrey

You can buy happiness and it's cheap.

~Tammy Strobel

> **"You should never get bored. There is a learning in every situation"**
>
> ~Raghavendra Prasad MG

It's not about saving Rs 10 by chasing a bus or Rs 100 by pursuing an auto. Life is a journey, and what you're chasing isn't the most important aspect. What truly matters is how passionate you are and how much enjoyment you derive from the pursuit.

> **"Money has no limit, but running after it can stress the brain. Instead, chase learning, and your brain will thrive"**

If you look at people who have achieved so much as authors, scientists, and more, you'll find that many of them lived well into their late 80s and 90s. It's their passion that allowed them to lead such long and fulfilling lives.

Ensure that you never experience stress in your present state. Whenever you do, it's essential to observe and analyse the situation:

Identify the Cause: Understand why you are feeling stressed, how long it has been bothering you, and its potential long-term or short-term impact.

Take Action: Work on getting out of the stressful state and return to a state of calm and comfort.

Feeling comfortable should be your constant state of being. If you ever find yourself stressed, it indicates a potential issue with your mindset. Take a moment to analyse why you might be feeling stressed. The reasons could include:

• Interactions with people • Challenging situations • Unfortunate events • Insecurity | Dependence on others • Loss | An unstable life	• Reactions to people's behavior • Excessive emotional attachment • Overprotectiveness • And more

By identifying the root cause of stress and addressing it, you can work towards maintaining a consistent state of comfort and tranquillity.

"Imagine you disappeared for 6 months. People would start to accept that you are not there to take care of their needs. If you disappeared for 2 years, they would have learned to live without you. If you were to reappear after 2 years, they might even feel uncomfortable breaking their current routine. This is how life is. So, remain calm, be comfortable, and shoulder your responsibilities without stress or ego as long as you are here. **Remember Everything is Replaceable on the Earth"**

"I have personally witnessed the passing of one of my friends who died at the age of 29 due to sudden cardiac arrest. Out of his 1500+ friends on Facebook, only four attended his funeral. Additionally, on the same day, he was removed from the WhatsApp group. This is a stark reflection of the reality of life. **Remember You are most important than anyone on this Earth"** - Make your comfortable among all situations you get in to.

> You have Complete Freedom, Take responsible &
> self-controlled (Disciplined) decisions.

> "In a calm state of mind, you can set & achieve
> realistic goals in life."
> ~Raghavendra Prasad MG

Couple of sayings from the experienced people, proverbs or philosophical teachings in the context of this chapter,

"To live a long life, one must be wise in the art of living."
~ Marcus Tullius Cicero

"A long life may not be good enough, but a good life is long enough."
~Benjamin Franklin

"The key to long life is avoiding becoming a burden to others."
~ Japanese Proverb

"To enjoy good health, to bring true happiness to one's family, to bring peace to all, one must first discipline and control one's own mind. If a man can control his mind, he can find the way to Enlightenment, and all wisdom and virtue will naturally come to him."
~Buddha

"Incorporate both the Fusion (Process happens on Sun) and Fission (Reaction while Atomic Bombing) concepts of Universe into your life to lead a successful and fulfilling life."

– As shown in the below diagrams,

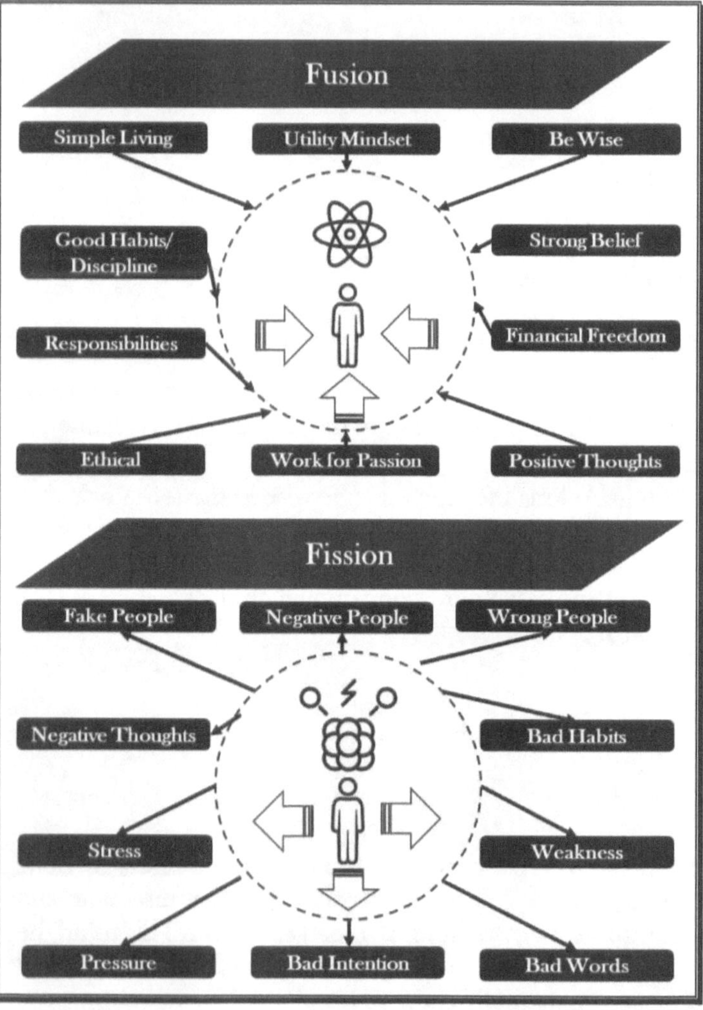

Personal Notes & Learnings

Personal Notes & Learnings

CHAPTER#18:
Intelligence vs. Wisdom - A Chapter for Making Meaningful Decisions

"Intelligence can be learned, but wisdom must be lived."

"The only true wisdom is in knowing you know nothing."
~Socrates

In this chapter, we'll explore the distinction between intelligence and wisdom which helps you in making significant life decisions in a right way.

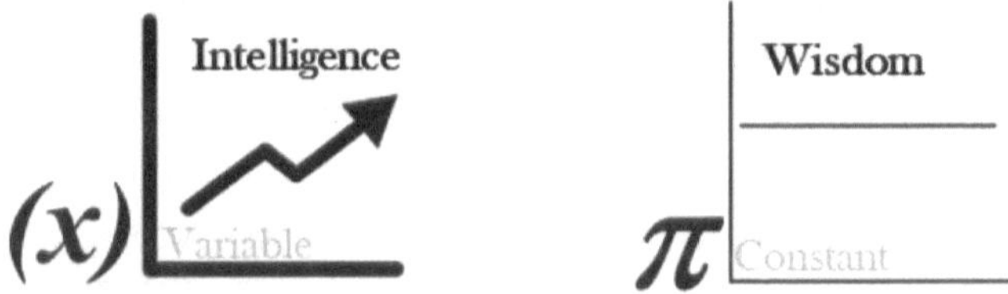

Intelligence && Wisdom in a Nutshell,

Intelligence	Wisdom
Understanding the world and others is Intelligence	knowing yourself is wisdom.
Intelligence is variable + demanding. Intelligence requires to be in race + Speed, constant upgrade required	Wisdom is constant + Immortal/ Eternal No Competition, Slow & Steady, Calm state
Used for personal (Selfish), Organizational, Country or a particular Community benefit & Growth – it might result bad or negative impact, side effects on others side or even earth as well.	Generous, It's good for all – Mankind, Nature, welfare to society, Earth, etc.., No Side effects.
Subset of Wisdom	Superset of Intelligence

"Intelligence is the ability to solve problems. Wisdom is the ability to avoid them, it's crucial to have intelligence with Wisdom."

Let's have a glance on couple of mantras written 1000's of years ago in Upanishads & Veda's which emphasizes the wisdom more than intelligence,

---

Annapoorneswari mantra

अन्नपूर्णे सदापूर्णे शङ्करप्राणवल्लभे ज्ञानवैराग्यसिद्ध्यर्थं भिक्षां देहि च पार्वति

"Annapoorne Sadapoorne Shankarpraanvallabhe Gyanvairagyasiddhyartham Bhavathi Bhikshandehicha Parvati"

The mantra is all about, **"Asking for wisdom and detachment as blessings for spiritual growth and understanding."**

Hayagriva mantra

ज्ञानानन्द मयं देवं निर्मल स्फटिकाकृतिं आधारं सर्वविद्यानं हयग्रीवं उपास्महे

"Gnanananda Mayam Devam Nirmala Spatika Kruthim Aadharam Sarva Vidyanam Hayagrivam Upasmahe"

The mantra all about asking for **"knowledge & wisdom"**

What Krishna says on wisdom?
नहीं जननेना सदृशं
"Nahi Gnanena Sadrusham"

It means, **"Without Wisdom one does not exist."**

Saraswathi mantra
सरस्वति नमस्तुभ्यं वरदे कामरूपिणि ।
|| विद्यारम्भं करिष्यामि सिद्धिर्भवतु मे सदा ||" Saraswati Namasthubhyam. Varade Kamarupini. Vidhyarambam Karishyami Siddhir Bavathume Sadha." It means, **"Asking goddess Saraswathi for blessing knowledge (Wisdom)"**

विनाशकाले विपरीतबुद्धि
"Vinashakale vipareetha Buddhi"

It means, **"High Intelligence leads to Destruction, Intelligence with wisdom is important"**

& So, on....!

If you observe all these mantras, you will notice that none of them emphasize intelligence explicitly. Instead, they all highlight the importance and significance of wisdom and knowledge in one's life.

Consider the potential for significant harm to humanity and the Earth due to advanced AI technologies, such as Artificial **Intelligence** (AI) and Generative Artificial **Intelligence** (GenAI).

"Intelligence may yield immediate outcomes, whether good or bad, while wisdom tends to lead to long-term positive results. Intelligence without Wisdom leads to Destruction"

~Raghavendra Prasad MG

"Intelligence alone can go wrong, but Wisdom never"
~Raghavendra Prasad MG

"Humans may create Artificial Intelligence, but they can never create Artificial Wisdom or knowledge. Therefore, being wise with intelligence is irreplaceable."

~Raghavendra Prasad MG

> Intelligence is crucial for survival in today's life, but wisdom is essential for long-term vision and enduring effects.
> ~Raghavendra Prasad MG

"Earning too much can signify a greater potential to harm or damage Mother Earth. Remember, the Earth is not in a hurry; it has taken 4.5 billion years to design humans on this planet. Let's avoid harming it and, instead, take time to relax and enjoy the journey of a purposeful life."

~Raghavendra Prasad MG

You can check for yourself; over 70-80% of your earnings may contribute to harming Mother Earth, either directly or indirectly. Aside from necessities like food, minimal clothing, and basic shelter, most other expenses are considered detrimental to the Earth.

How Do Intelligent and People with Wisdom Look at and Think About Various Aspects of Life?

Summary is depicted in the below table,

Object	Intelligence View	Wisdom View
Nature	Seek for the opportunities	Appreciate the creation
People	Mostly based on Financial & Social Status	As a Human Being, accept as he/she is with respect
Money	How can I add more or multiply? Let me invest Increase my social showoffs	It's just a paper and how much is required for me Let me give, do charity, good deeds Let me spend time Spiritually, and try to understand the purpose of life.
Problem handling	Opportunities, Profits Expert in gauging others	Route Cause and long-term, ethical solutions without selfishness
Earth	I am the owner mindset, Earth Gets Damaged	I am the visitor, Earth Gets Flourished
Peace	Searching outside	He knows its inside
Financial Status	Enjoyment, Comfort living,	Temporary, don't care
Identity	Achievement, Recognition	Temporary, don't care
Materialistic thinking	Better quality, brand	Utility mindset
Listening to others	To Reply, Accept, React, Respond, bring Point of View, etc.	To Learn, nothing to prove or disprove, everyone is right in their point of view.

Living & Learning	Learn to Live, feel the complexity in life	Live to Learn, has clarity in life
Mental State	Mostly Restless, Running Mode	Calm & Constant mindset
Happiness	Outside	Inside
Vision	Can See today & decision are taken based on the current moment benefit	Can See Future & decisions be taken based on the future based and moral and ethical thoughts
Decision Parameters	Cognitive ability, problem-solving skills, analytical, logical, and critical thinking Quick in decisions making	Deep understanding about life, nature, true knowledge, empathy, ethical, compassion, emotional. Slow in decisions making
Life	Life comes once, enjoy, keep high expectation, try to get everything possible, go behind comfort, etc., leads a Comfort life.	Life is a journey enjoy it; expectations are like baggage's. hence lesser the baggage very easy to move forward, leads a Quality life.
Relationships	Mutual interest and benefit	Mutual respect and values
Success	Career & financial growth or gains	Matured to be well-being, personal growth through purposeful learnings, contributions to the society for a good cause.

Living Style	Materialistic life with Comfort, Dependency	Simple with utility mindset, Self-Dependent
Effect and Outcome	Immediate	Delayed, Long-term impact
Relationship Between Intelligence & Wisdom	Intelligence is a Subset of Wisdom	Wisdom is a superset of Intelligence
	Having Only Intelligence is very dangerous.	One can't have Wisdom without Intelligence.

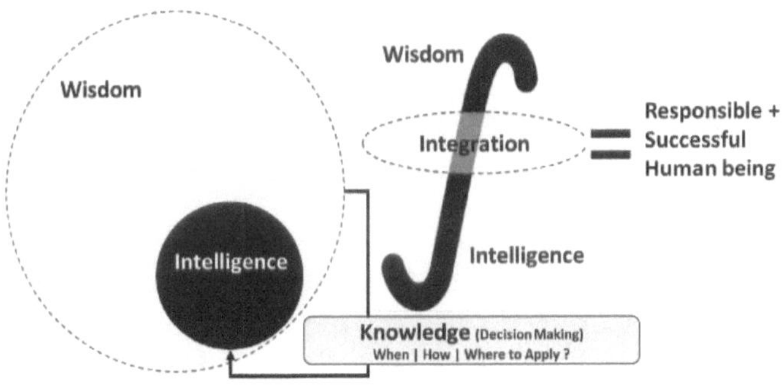

Couple of sayings from the experienced people, proverbs or philosophical teachings in the context of this chapter,

"Wisdom comes from reflection."

~Deborah Day

"A fool thinks himself to be wise, but a wise man knows himself to be a fool."

~William Shakespeare

"Wisdom is not a product of schooling but of the lifelong attempt to acquire it."

~Albert Einstein

"Knowing others is intelligence; knowing yourself is true wisdom. Mastering others is strength; mastering yourself is true power."

~Lao Tzu

"Wisdom begins in wonder."

~Socrates

"The more wisdom you attain and the more conscious you become, the crazier you will appear to others."

~Deepak Chopra

"The invariable mark of wisdom is to see the miraculous in the common."

~Ralph Waldo Emerson

"By three methods we may learn wisdom: First, by reflection, which is noblest; Second, by imitation, which is easiest; and third by experience, which is the bitterest."

~Confucius

"It is the province of knowledge to speak, and it is the privilege of wisdom to listen."

~Oliver Wendell Holmes Sr.

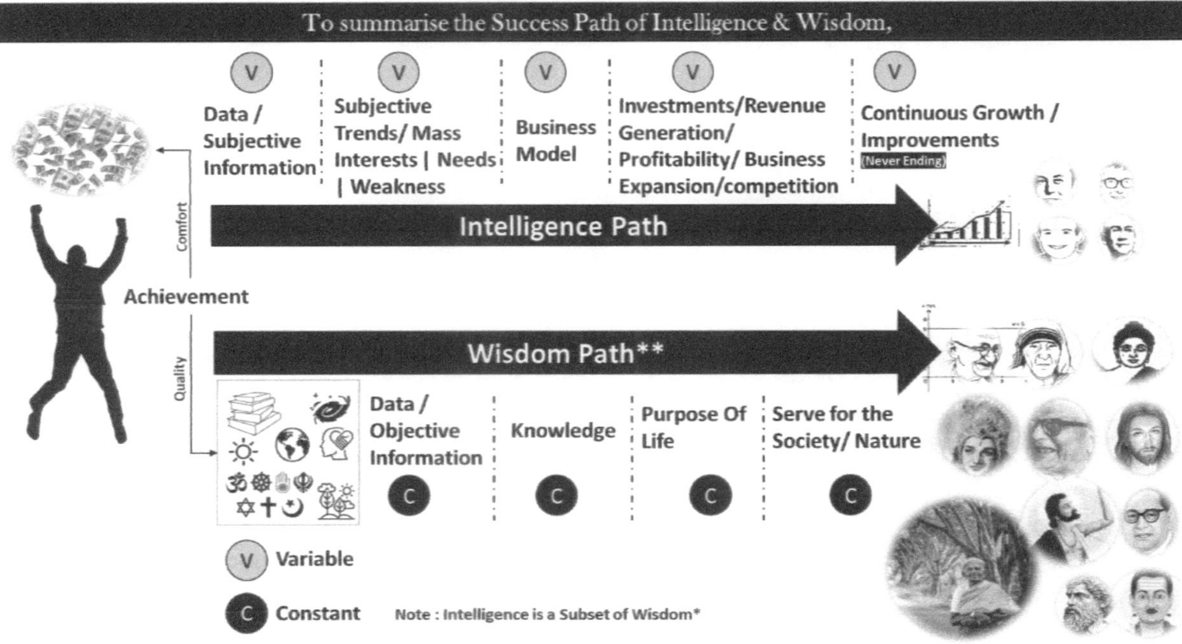
To summarise the Success Path of Intelligence & Wisdom,
Data / Subjective Information
Subjective Trends/ Mass Interests | Needs | Weakness
Business Model
Investments/Revenue Generation/ Profitability/ Business Expansion/competition
Continuous Growth / Improvements
(Never Ending)
Intelligence Path
Comfort
Achievement
Quality
Wisdom Path**
Data / Objective Information
Knowledge
Purpose Of Life
Serve for the Society/ Nature
V Variable
C Constant
Note : Intelligence is a Subset of Wisdom*

Personal Notes & Learnings

CONCLUSION

"At the end of the day, everything reaches an equilibrium state. What you possess today was once owned by someone else yesterday, and it will inevitably pass on to someone else tomorrow. Life is inherently impermanent. Therefore, it's crucial to find relaxation & joy in the journey of life. Let's cultivate wisdom, simple living, discover a meaningful purpose in life with good intentions, practice kindness, continue to experience and learn as long as we walk on this Earth — use minimum resources, all without harming our Mother Earth. We must ensure that we pass it on to the next generation as it was passed to us by our ancestors."

~Raghavendra Prasad MG

"Chapters" V/S "Concept Mapping"

PREFACE				
#	Math	Science	Analytics	Art
Ch#01				
Ch#02				
Ch#03				
Ch#04				
Ch#05				
Ch#06				
Ch#07				
Ch#08				
Ch#09				
Ch#10				
Ch#11				
Ch#12				
Ch#13				
Ch#14				
Ch#15				
Ch#16				
Ch#17				
Ch#18				
CONCLUSION				

Author Consultation & Counseling:

I won't necessarily solve all your life problems, but you can contact me for consultation or counseling to gain my Point of View (POV) on the challenges and issues you feel in your life.
My perspective may help you handle these problems more efficiently.

Email: YourReflectionYourGod@gmail.com

Thanks,
Dr. Raghavendra Prasad MG

ACKNOWLEDGEMENTS

I would like to thank the universe for the health, Right Thought Process, Opportunities, Prosperity, Abundance, Guidance, and Blessings in my life.

I would like to thank my parents who served, educated me, and provided me a path to success.

I would like to thank all of my friends, especially the elderly friends, who taught me lots of valuable lessons and provided guidance.

I would like to express my gratitude to Notion Press for helping me share my thoughts with readers around the world through this book.